The
Weekly
Feeder

The Weekly Feeder

A Revolutionary Shopping,

Cooking, & Meal Planning System

Cori Kirkpatrick

STARBURST PUBLISHERS®

P. O. Box 4123, Lancaster, Pennsylvania 17604

To schedule author appearances, write:

Author Appearances
Starburst Promotions
P.O. Box 4123,
Lancaster, Pennsylvania 17604
or call (717) 293-0939

www.starburstpublishers.com

CREDITS:
Cover design by David Marty Designs
Cover photo by Joy Schaffert
Text design and composition by John Reinhardt Book Design

First Printing, November, 1999

ISBN: 1-892016-09-5
Library of Congress Catalog Number: 99-63791
Printed in the United States of America

Dedication

To John

For 30 years of laughter, too many rewards to count
and his gentle, relentless nudge.

To Brad, Justin, Jill, and Julie

For their appreciation and encouragement.
They are our world.

To my Dad

For his sharp pencil, and so much more.

To Nan and Toots

Who showed me how to season with love.

I'd also like to thank a group of wonderful women whose thoughtful advice and ideas added breadth to the scope of the book. They include Wendy Crocker, Terri Kimball, Susan Adkins, Sue Cary, Shelley Larkins, Sandy Gannan, Peggy Stamm, Peggy Gordon, Pat Thirlby, Nina Fogg, Mary Rae Cowles, Marty Weiden, Leilia Pierce, Kandie Holmberg, Jean Amick, Jane Summerfelt, Gail Ransom, Jackie Bradley, Jane Brand, Helen Schaa, Dinny Polson, Cindy Freimuth, Jane Cancro, Carrie Dodobara, Bobbi Benson, Kathy Kane, Barbara Kirk, Anne Zubko, Tracy Quigley, Suzy Keeler, Sue Hansen, Annette Reiger, Beverly Fuhs, Chris Carpenter, Cindy Henderson, Jane Galliher, Janet Huguenin, Carol Rhodes, Karen Michel, Judy Curran, Laurie Schuchart, Linda Jensen, Mary O'Donnell, Marybeth Alwood, Pat Fitzgerald, Patty Lakamp, Peggy Hanel, Penny Lewis, Sue Bohman, Margo Stevenson, Penny Fredlund, Burnley Snyder, Colleen Roland, Sheila Magnano, Jackie Mansfield, and Karen Harris.

Contents

Follow the arrows to a delicious dinner!

Choose one of eight weekly menu options that the author has prepared . . .

1

Tear out the corresponding grocery list that the author has already made for you . . .

2

Zip in and out of the grocery store . . .

3

Check for "staple items" that are out-of-stock in your pantry and add any necessary personal items to your list . . .

4

The hard part is done . . . the author saved you time by doing all of the planning for you! Now sit back, relax, and think about actually ENJOYING cooking for a week!

Each night choose a dinner recipe that sounds appealing or incorporate your own recipes with the author's easy instructions . . .

5

Enjoy a relaxed, well-balanced meal with your family . . . with virtually no hassle . . .

Now the easy part . . . Get out of the kitchen and on with the rest of your life!

Place your healthy and delicious meal on the table in less than 45 minutes . . .

Follow one simple recipe to prepare main dish, salad, and vegetable or side . . .

The Weekly Feeder meal and menu planning system is designed to help busy people find time to enjoy healthy, home-cooked meals with the ones they love! So instead of hitting the drive-thru or stressing out over "What's for dinner?" try **The Weekly Feeder**!

The author has already done the work for you by pre-planning 8 weeks of dinner menus. In fact, she has also made out the grocery lists and even organized them to follow the layout of the average grocery store . . . how easy is that?

Now you can make mealtime special again with **The Weekly Feeder** from Starburst Publishers!

Introduction

I never planned to write a cookbook. When I devised this meal-planning system twelve years ago, I did it to simplify my own life. I had just gone back to work and had a typical assortment of other commitments, plus cooking responsibilities for my busy physician/husband and three active, athletic adolescents. They weren't picky eaters, but they definitely cared about what they ate.

You may share the cooking chores, or be a single dad or a full-time working mom. Everyone's circumstances are different, but we're all similarly over-committed, and that's why this timesaving concept is appealing.

The nagging 4:00 P.M. "What's for dinner tonight?" question was my nemesis. I wanted to offer my family nutritious, varied dinners, but I didn't have the time to plan, shop, and prepare them on a daily basis. I enjoyed the hands-on part of cooking—the chopping and slicing, tossing a bright mix of greens in a clean glass bowl. It was just deciding what to prepare, and then purchasing the ingredients, that I found tedious and time-consuming. I was not—and am not—a gourmet cook, but I do enjoy fresh, healthy ingredients prepared with a little flair.

The idea for this meal-planning system occurred to me on a Saturday morning run and I spent all my spare time that weekend creating four "WEEKS" out of my favorite recipes. It was so simple and logical that I couldn't wait to test how well it worked. And work it did! That was twelve years ago and I've been using the very same system ever since, with revisions and additions as kids come and go. I can't imagine cooking without it, as it has truly eased my stress, added more free time, and created more pleasant family mealtime moments than anything else I have ever done.

For years my husband and children urged me to publish this book. The original copy is in a food-splattered plastic binder that I still use. Over the years John has photocopied sections of it for patients, as I have done for friends and work acquaintances. But the time has now come to share it, so other families can experience the pleasures and benefits of eating together and eating well—with a minimum of planning and effort. This is how!

Learning the System

Since Eve ate apples, man depends on dinner.
—Lord Byron

How It Works

More than ever, our calendars are full and our days are a dizzy blur of activity. Aside from work and family, we have committee meetings and sporting events, laundry, weeds, and bills, birthday presents and holiday decorations, thank-you notes and emails, car repairs and new shoes, potluck suppers and charitable donations, stairclimbers and treadmills, a good book or two, and the fun of planning a well-deserved vacation. The list goes on and on . . . and THEN we're supposed to have dinner ready? The volume and variety of things to do can be overwhelming, and adults as well as children feel the stress of today's typical American lifestyle.

How nice it would be if dinnertime were an oasis from such busyness—a time of ease, security, and togetherness. No daily planning, no hurried trips to the grocery store, just the quick preparation of simple, fresh meals using ingredients that you purchased in one time-saving trip to the grocery store. That's the *Weekly Feeder* plan. The emphasis in this cookbook is on simplicity of ingredients and preparation—of cooking meals that are appealing to the eye, the palate, the heart, and the pocketbook. And the delightful result is that you will not only enjoy a more pleasant dinner hour, but you'll have more time for all those things you would much rather do than shop for groceries and cook!

Every time you prepare dinner there are three steps involved. First, you must plan what to cook. Second, you need to check your refrigerator and cupboards to see if you have the necessary ingredients on hand, and then make a trip to the grocery store for those you don't have. The third step is the actual preparation. The *Weekly Feeder* system saves time and effort with two of those steps. Not only does it totally eliminate the meal-planning—that has already been done for you—but it significantly reduces the time spent grocery shopping by consolidating numerous weekly trips to the store into one. You are now left with the one step that can actually be fun, if you haven't spent extra time on the other two.

The basic concept behind the *Weekly Feeder* system is simple: you make one trip to the grocery store to purchase all the ingredients you need to prepare five family dinners for the week. Everything you need is included in this book: well-balanced lists of healthy meals that are quick and easy to prepare; the grocery lists necessary to prepare those meals; and, of course, the recipes.

The system is based on a plan of eight separate, unique "WEEKS," with WEEK 8 offering meals for special events. Each of the eight WEEKS contains the following elements:

- A list of five complete dinner menus for that WEEK
- The recipes to prepare those five dinner menus
- A grocery list of the ingredients needed to prepare the five dinners for that WEEK

Read on to see just how easily those elements work together to simplify your dinner planning and preparation.

The Dinner Menus

The five dinner menus included in each of the eight different WEEKS were planned with variety, balance, good nutrition, and ease of preparation in mind. Each contains an interesting mix of chicken, beef, and seafood entrees, although you'll probably notice that chicken entrees outnumber beef and seafood about 2:1. It's a rare week that has more than one beef entree.

Each dinner menu is nutritionally balanced, containing a protein source, a starch, usually more than one vegetable, and often fruit. For the most part the recipes are quick and easy entrees that don't require a lot of complicated preparation. Once you become familiar with the preparation steps and adept at the chopping and slicing, few meals will take more than 45 minutes total preparation time. And remember that the preparation time won't be extended by any extra time spent planning the meal or shopping for missing ingredients.

From among the five dinners in a WEEK, what you choose to serve on any particular night is up to you. There's no pre-determined or necessary sequence to the five meals. I usually prepare the seafood entree on Monday or Tuesday so that the fish can be eaten when it's most fresh. Or I'll save a dinner that's particularly quick to prepare for a night when I know I'll be coming home late and will have less time than usual to cook the evening meal.

It's important to remember that each of the eight WEEKS contains only five dinners because there are usually two nights a week when you're doing other things. Even if your social calendar is quiet, every cook deserves an occasional break from kitchen responsibilities, and nothing tastes better than a cheesy, thick-crust pizza once in a while!

The Recipes

You'll notice immediately that the format of these recipes looks different than those in other cookbooks. That's because each *Weekly Feeder* dinner recipe incorporates all the items in the entire meal—the entree, accompaniments and salad—and thus is actually 3-recipes-in-1 or even 4-in-1. In other words, the ingredient lists and preparation steps for three or four different recipes have been combined into a single *Weekly Feeder* recipe, coordinating preparation of the entire meal, and ensuring that all the menu items will be ready to place on your table at the same time.

Although the idea of combining three or four recipes may sound complicated and the recipes can look long and involved at first glance, they are actually extremely easy to read, understand, and follow. Each recipe follows the same format. Take WEEK 3 for example. There is one single recipe that combines the ingredient lists and preparation steps for a dinner menu of Angel Hair Pasta with Crab, Green Salad, and French Bread. This means your entire meal can be prepared simultaneously and every dish is ready at the same time. No time or effort is lost!

The Grocery Lists

The grocery list for each WEEK is the key to the system, and each grocery list contains every ingredient necessary to prepare all five dinners for that particular WEEK. For your convenience, the Appendix in the back of the book contains extra copies of the grocery lists for all eight WEEKS, perforated for easy removal. In addition, each WEEK contains a master grocery list that can be photocopied at a later date.

The groceries are listed in two sections. Items on the front of the list are mostly fresh ingredients that you will use that WEEK in their entirety (¾ pound of lean ground beef or two large onions, for example). Items on the back are the spices, condiments, and other staples that you may already have on hand and will only use a small amount of. Notice that the items on the back are listed under the word "CHECK." Once you select your WEEK and pull the corresponding grocery list from the book, you should go down those items in the CHECK column and place a mark next to the ones that aren't already in your cupboard or refrigerator. Those items you will need to purchase.

Once you begin using this system, you'll discover that the order of items in the grocery list for each WEEK is also planned to save time. If you visit a number of different grocery stores, you'll see that the floor layout is similar from one store to the next. Fresh items are usually on the outside walls, with canned and prepared goods in the middle aisles. To make your *Weekly Feeder* shopping more efficient, the grocery list for each WEEK is arranged to follow the aisles in a typical grocery store so that you can start at the top of the list and move more quickly to the bottom. The aisles of your favorite local market may not follow the exact sequence, but the grocery lists should be close enough to the floor plan of your favorite store to pleasantly simplify your shopping.

The one item on the grocery lists that may cause some confusion is boneless, skinned chicken breasts, which are a frequent ingredient in *Weekly Feeder* recipes because they are nutritious, easy to prepare, and work well with so many other interesting foods and flavors. If a grocery list or recipe lists "4 boneless, skinned chicken breasts," this means four "½ breast" or single serving portions. Most likely, you will find this amount pre-packaged in the meat department of your favorite store with a total weight of approximately 1.25 to 1.50 pounds of chicken.

The variation in the weight of chicken breasts underscores the fact that these recipes are very flexible. While the recipes will generally serve four hungry adults, you can increase the number of people you can serve—or the portion size—by increasing the amount of pasta you use, by adding an extra chicken breast, or by tossing more broccoli into the stir fry. With experience, you will tailor the recipes to best suit your family.

Applying the System to Your Recipes

As you go through this cookbook, keep in mind that the emphasis is on the *system* and not on the recipes themselves. Your own favorite recipes can easily be adapted to this format, and I encourage you to do so. The last chapter in the book is called "Making a Plan Your Own," and it will take you step-by-step through the process of creating your own personal WEEKS using your family's favorite recipes. As you study the book and sample some of the WEEKS, keep notes on recipes of your own that would work well together as part of your own personal *Weekly Feeder* system.

The Equipment

When we moved into our house twelve years ago, I knew we would be remodeling the tiny kitchen within a year. Because of that, I unpacked only the necessities to make our temporary kitchen functional. Twelve years have passed and I haven't unpacked the extra boxes yet. Instead, those duplicate mixing bowls, casseroles of every size and shape, and other extraneous items have been passed along to my kids as they moved away from home and set up housekeeping on their own. I've learned from experience that it's actually more efficient to limit the equipment and supplies in your kitchen to what you regularly use.

What follows is a list of basic kitchen equipment used to prepare *Weekly Feeder* dinners and desserts. If you've been the chief cook for a while, you may already have accumulated most of these items. If you're setting up a kitchen for the first time, remember that it's worth investing in good quality equipment because of its durability and ease of use.

Knives are the most essential item and should be carefully cared for and stored. Most people prefer high-carbon stainless-steel knives but, whatever your choice, be sure to include a sharpener and use it!

Pots and pans can be found in several different materials. This is really up to your personal preference, but I like to use pots and pans with a non-stick surface because they're easier to clean. Some people prefer stainless steel with aluminum or copper bases, enamel-coated cast iron, or glass ceramic that can go from the stovetop to the microwave or directly into the oven. The beauty and function of copper appeals to other cooks, although copper takes more time and effort to care for.

As long as you make educated, well-researched choices you should be happy with the equipment that you purchase.

KNIVES

1	paring knife—3½ inches	1	carving knife—10 inches
1	cook's knife—6 inches	1	serrated bread knife–10 inches
1	chef's knife—8 inches	1	sharpening steel

POTS, PANS, AND SERVING DISHES

2	saucepots—2½ quart and 5 quart	1	Dutch oven or casserole— 3 quart with a lid
1	stockpot—8 quart, with tight-fitting lid	1	microwave-safe glass ceramic casserole with a lid
1	frying pan—10 inches (preferably non-stick)	1	large salad bowl
1	large wok (preferably non-stick)	1	decorative bowl for fruit

UTENSILS

1	bottle opener	2	long-handled wooden spoons
1	bulb baster	6	measuring cups for dry ingredients (¼ cup, ⅓ cup, ½ cup, ⅔ cup ¾ cup, and 1 cup)
1	heavy-duty can opener		
1	citrus juicer	3	glass measuring cups for liquids (1 cup, 2 cup, and 4 cup)
1	citrus zester		
1	colander (preferably stainless steel, with legs)	1	set of measuring spoons
2	large cutting boards (I prefer lucite, others prefer wood)	1	meat thermometer
		1	metal spatula
1	garlic press	1	set of 4 nested mixing bowls
1	ice cream scoop	1	pepper grinder
1	kitchen timer	2	rubber spatulas
1	kitchen tongs	1	salad spinner
		1	soup ladle

1	kitchen shears	1	spaghetti fork or pasta server
1	long-handled fork	1	standing 4-sided grater
1	long-handled stainless-steel slotted spoon	1	vegetable peeler
1	long-handled stainless-steel spoon	1	wire whisk

BAKING EQUIPMENT

2	round cake pans, 9 inches	1	rimless baking sheet
1	springform pan, 9 inches	1	ovenproof glass pie plate
1	rectangular baking pan, 13 x 9 inches	1	muffin tin, 12 cups with ½ cup capacity
1	glass ceramic baking dish, 13 x 9 inches	1	flour sifter
1	square baking pan, 9 inches	1	heavy rolling pin
1	loaf pan, 9 x 5 x 3 inches	1	wire rack
1	fluted tart pan with removable bottom, 10 inches x 1 inch deep	1	pastry brush
2	rimmed baking sheets, 18 x 12 x 1	1	candy thermometer
		1	set of cookie cutters

ELECTRIC EQUIPMENT

1	hand mixer	1	microwave oven, 650 to 700 watts
1	standing mixer, 4- to 5-quart capacity	1	double oven (desirable)
1	food processor, 7-cup capacity		

Staple Foods

The grocery list for each WEEK includes a column under the heading "CHECK" that lists staples required for that WEEK's menus. You are likely to already have many of these staples in your refrigerator or on your pantry shelves. The following is a summary of the spices, condiments, oils, sauces, and basic ingredients compiled from the CHECK columns of all eight grocery lists. If you are a beginning cook it would be costly to purchase all of these items at once, but as your experience in the kitchen grows and you try out more *Weekly Feeder* WEEKS, you will soon accumulate all of the staple items on this list.

OILS, SAUCES, CONDIMENTS, ETC.

balsamic vinegar	flour
brown sugar	honey
butter/margarine	ketchup
chicken bouillon	light mayonnaise
cornstarch	light soy sauce
Dijon mustard	Madeira
dry breadcrumbs	mirin (sweet rice wine)
eggs	

SPICES

basil	ground ginger
bay leaf	marjoram
celery seed	oregano
chili powder	rosemary
crushed red pepper	salt and pepper
cumin	thyme
curry powder	toasted sesame seeds
garlic powder	whole black peppercorns
garlic salt	

How the System Can Improve Health

"You are what you eat." In recent years the scientific community has emphasized that premise, while bombarding us with a dizzying amount of information on the merits (and, more frequently, the demerits) of countless foods. It often seems that just about anything we put in our mouths other than pure fresh water is bad for us. Wait. Is that water fluoridated?

Now it seems that the healthy lifestyle pendulum is swinging back to the merits of a balanced diet emphasizing moderation, paired with a regular exercise program, to maintain optimum good health and energy. Healthy living really means using good common sense, following certain basic principles in food selection and preparation, planning your discretionary time to permit sustained strenuous exercise on a regular basis, and maintaining a positive mental attitude. By consistently adhering to a few some simple guidelines, we will more likely be healthy and happy, inside and out.

GUIDELINE #1

Eat a variety of foods each day from the four food groups,
including a generous amount of fruits, vegetables,
and whole grain breads and cereals:

Grain products	5–12 servings per day
Vegetables and fruit	5–10 servings per day
Milk products	2–4 servings per day
Meat and alternatives	
(poultry, fish, legumes, nuts)	2–3 servings per day

A balanced diet is necessary to insure adequate intake of the vitamins required for good health. Food is a better way to obtain your vitamins than pills because food provides vitamins in the most biologically-available form, in the right amounts and combined with other complementary nutrients.

A balanced diet contains not only the vitamins necessary for good health, but also the fiber required for good digestion. A major benefit of fiber is that you may actually consume less, because high-fiber foods are bulky, take longer to chew, and make you feel full. Fiber is found not only in the bran cereal or the whole wheat toast you eat for breakfast, but is present in all sorts of vegetables—like broccoli, corn and spinach—and in your favorite fruits like apples, bananas, cantaloupe, and pears. Even some of the snack foods you enjoy, like dates and prunes, are actually very high in fiber.

GUIDELINE #2

Select, prepare, and serve foods with limited amounts
of fat, sugar, and salt.

Let's examine those three elements individually.

FAT—While small amounts of fat are needed each day to maintain good health, most people consume more than is necessary. Fat becomes part of your daily diet in three ways. It is found naturally in meat and milk products; it is added during food processing in most commercially baked goods, candy bars, snack foods, and processed meats; and it is also added during food preparation in the form of butter or margarine, sour cream, sauces, and salad dressings.

But eating less fat doesn't necessarily mean meals have to be tasteless and dull. You can make small, simple changes in your daily fat consumption by choosing foods that are lower in fat, by using cooking methods such as broiling, stir frying, and steaming instead of old-fashioned frying, and by adding table fats in moderation. It's the little things. Trim the visible fat off of meat and remove the skin from chicken, add a teaspoon of butter to your bread or vegetables rather than a tablespoon, choose light sour cream and skim milk instead of the high-fat variety, and drain your bacon on a paper towel. Use mono-unsaturated oils (olive, peanut, or canola) or polyunsaturated (safflower, sesame, or corn) rather than saturated (coconut or palm) in your cooking. These small, easy steps can make the difference in lowering your total fat consumption.

SUGAR—Sugar provides energy and perks up the flavor of foods and again, when used in moderation, can be part of a healthy diet. Like fat, sugar occurs naturally in some foods such as fruits. Sugar is also added during food processing to sweet baked goods, candy bars, snack foods, pop, and fruit drinks, and we all add sugar during food preparation or at the table in the form of white or brown sugar, syrup, honey, or jam.

Sugar has been blamed for medical conditions from obesity to diabetes to heart disease, and has also been blamed for social problems such as hyperactivity and delinquent behavior. But the scientific research is inconclusive, and a moderate approach to sugar consumption is likely best. As with lowering fat consumption, there are easy ways to limit our sugar intake as well. Drink water or unsweetened fruit juices instead of soda pop; limit the sugar on cereal and the syrup on pancakes; add chunks of fresh fruit to plain yogurt rather than eating the highly-sweetened, fruit-flavored yogurts; and reach for a whole-grain muffin rather than a doughnut at snack time. You can even experiment when you're baking; the sugar in a recipe can be reduced by ⅓ without ruining the finished product.

SALT—As with fat and sugar, salt can be consumed in moderation as part of a healthy diet. But salt can be more harmful to some of us than others, and excess sodium can actually cause high blood pressure and potentially heart disease and stroke. For this reason it is wise to limit your salt intake.

While the average adult only needs about 0.7 grams of sodium a day for good health, an intake of 6–7 grams is acceptable. Many people consume 10 to 20 times the amount of salt they need because of its prevalence in processed foods such as luncheon meats, popcorn, chips, processed "fast" foods such as commercially prepared main courses, pizza and tacos, and commercial soups, sauces, and condiments.

It's relatively easy to cut down on salt consumption by eating more fresh foods, by flavoring with lemon, pepper, vinegar, and garlic, by cooking fresh vegetables in the microwave rather than in salty water, and by omitting salt in the cooking water for pasta, rice, and potatoes. We can also take it easy on foods like pickles, salty snack foods, and prepared foods. Fresh is always best!

GUIDELINE #3

Exercise as often as you can and maintain flexibility.

I'm not an exercise fanatic, but I know that 20 to 30 minutes of sustained strenuous exercise three or four times a week is good for the heart, bones, muscles, and psyche. Exercise just makes you feel good! Plus, regular exercise can raise your resting metabolic rate—making weight control easier—and can lower cholesterol and blood pressure, keeping blood glucose levels steady and making the body's insulin more effective. In addition, exercise improves the strength of your muscles and, if the exercise is weight-bearing, works to build strong, dense bones as well.

Remember also that exercise is necessary, not only for developing aerobic fitness to keep your heart and lungs working well, but to keep your body supple and flexible. Don't forget the value of stretching and, as you inevitably get older, sign up for a yoga or stretch-and-tone class to improve your flexibility and keep your joints mobile and lubricated.

GUIDELINE #4

Make an effort to manage stress and maintain a positive attitude.

Stress, tension, and anxiety are a part of everyday life and have been linked as a causative factor in a long list of serious illnesses. We know that stress drains energy and can even damage the immune system. Ever notice how you are more likely to catch a cold when you're under pressure?

Vigorous exercise can help you deal with stress, but there are other approaches as well. Practice relaxation techniques or learn to meditate to create a feeling of calm and an ability to cope. Pamper yourself with an occasional special treat or "escape" like an afternoon at the movies. Make an effort to spent at least ten minutes outdoors, especially during wintertime. The brisk, bracing fresh air will help ward off a lack of energy and the depression that can result from the very real loss of light during those gray winter months.

Life *isn't* always easy but it will be easier if your attitude is optimistic rather than pessimistic. Don't waste time agonizing over situations or individuals that you are unable to change. If you learn to accept your circumstances and determine to make the best of them, you'll find that you enjoy things more—and will be both happier and *healthier* as a result.

GUIDELINE #5

Drink plenty of fresh water.

This is an easy one. Keep a glass of water by your desk or on the table and try to drink up to eight glasses a day. You'll be amazed how good it makes you feel!

Will the *Weekly Feeder* system help you follow these simple guidelines? The answer is a resounding "yes!" It can reduce the stress in your life by making meal-planning and preparation much easier and will create more discretionary time that you can spend getting some vigorous exercise or share with family and friends.

Most important, you can enjoy the meals in this cookbook, confident that your diet meets good nutritional standards. You'll notice that at the end of each recipe is a list of the percentages of the meal's calories that come from protein, carbohydrate, and fat. While the typical American diet currently contains 15 to 18% of total calories from protein, 40 to 50% from fat (mostly saturated), and 30 to 40% from carbohydrates (mostly refined), it's better to aim for a different balance. With an emphasis on increasing carbohydrates and decreasing fat, try to eat 15 to 20% of your calories from protein, around 30% of your calories from fat (only ⅓ saturated), and 55 to 60% of your calories from mostly unrefined carbohydrates.

But one important word of caution: while most meals in this cookbook are appropriately balanced, not every one falls within the desirable percentages. It's important to recognize—and even savor—the fact that the reason we eat food is not only to sustain life, but for pleasure and enjoyment. Just as it's OK to miss an exercise session occasionally, it's also OK once in a while to prepare and enjoy a sauce made with (yes!) real heavy cream. Why? Because its smooth richness just tastes good.

A Last Word Before You Begin

It's hard to resist the opportunity to express some personal philosophy.

First, a confession. The true impetus behind the *Weekly Feeder* system was not just a wish to organize and simplify my life. What I really wanted was to create consistent, reliable (but easy on the cook) times for our family to be together, and dinner was the logical time. We all have to eat.

Placing a home-cooked meal on the table was something I wanted to do *for* my family, a subtle way to quietly let them know, day-in-and-out, how much I cared about them. It's the "comfort food" concept. Handing your hungry teenage son a warm plate piled high with his favorite pasta—its steaming, zesty aroma tempting his always-ravenous appetite—communicates a special message. Handing him a cardboard box of soggy pizza, an aluminum foil package of bland frozen food, or a brown paper bag of deli delight communicates something totally different. Gee, *thanks,* Mom.

We've all read research underscoring the difficulty of finding time in our fast-paced lives for families to be together. A 1995 Gallup poll found that less than ⅓ of the respondents ate dinner together on a regular basis. A University of Maryland study concluded that today's parents spend only 17 hours per week with their children, down 40% from 1965. Another nationwide study found that 66% of adults surveyed wanted more time with their kids.

The next step—drawing conclusions on the importance of "togetherness" in a child's emotional development—has been examined by other research. When 1500 school-aged children were recently asked what they thought made a happy family, the most frequent answer was "doing things together." Another study specifically linked teenagers' meals to their psychological adjustment, finding that teens who showed good psychological adjustment ate a meal with an adult family member an average of five days a week, compared to three days for teens who weren't as well adjusted. The researchers concluded that the reason might be as simple as showing the teenager that the adult cares enough about them to eat with them.

Are we coming full circle, back to finding wisdom in the old-fashioned values espoused by our mothers and mothers-in-law? Those women now in their 60s and older spent hours in the kitchen on a daily basis preparing meals for their families. (Who could ever forget mushroom soup casseroles?) Back then, family dinners were a given, a reliably pleasant respite at the end of each day. Through the preparation of food these women were expressing care and concern for those they loved, and in doing so fostered stable, secure families.

Granted, our worlds have expanded and life today is different. Our responsibilities are more complex, challenging, and time-consuming. Our families are frequently an ethnically diverse mix of ages and sexes. Dad often shares the cooking responsibilities with Mom . . . or he or she may be a single parent. But amidst the change is one constant human need, particularly in young people, for consistent expressions of caring.

I'd never claim that using the *Weekly Feeder* system will assure proper psychological adjustment of your children. But it is a small, easy way to work toward that goal, while at the same time helping yourself. Just think of the benefits to the cook! No more dashing to the grocery store in a rainstorm to pick up frozen lasagna. No more grimacing as the cash register totals your purchases at that upscale neighborhood deli. No more agonizing at work about whether there's *anything* in the refrigerator that could be thrown together and considered a meal.

The *Weekly Feeder* is a simple, easy way to care for those you care about.

Get Ready, Get Set, Go!

It's now Sunday afternoon or Monday morning, and you're ready to give the *Weekly Feeder* system a try. Start by looking at the different menus listed for each WEEK and choose a WEEK that looks appealing. Next, find the corresponding grocery list and remove it from the cookbook. You now need to go through the CHECK items on the back of the grocery list to make sure that you already have an ample supply of each staple ingredient in your refrigerator or pantry. Mark the ones that you don't have on hand and will need to purchase.

You'll notice that the pre-printed grocery lists also have a blank area where you can add other items that you need to purchase. Consider the next few days and add whatever you need for breakfasts, lunches, treats, laundry, etc., to the grocery list. You may also want to add more fruit for after-school snacks, some sweets for desserts, turkey for sandwiches, milk to drink, etc. As you become more familiar with the system, you can embellish the recipes as well, adding your own special touch. You may prefer other vegetables in your green salad, or perhaps some fruits. Don't be afraid to make changes—the stir fry recipes can be easily altered or augmented to suit your family's special preferences. If you're not a fan of zucchini, for example, you might want to toss some extra broccoli into the wok as a replacement and to add more color and crunch. If carrots are your daughter's favorite, add those, too.

Once the grocery list is personalized, you're ready to go. Plan on spending less than 45 minutes in the grocery store, again because the grocery list will relate to the floor plan of your favorite market. My record for a full week's shopping is 28 minutes. You'll find that most of your time will be spent in the produce department. To speed things up in that section, I always count up the number of plastic bags that I'll need and pull them off all at once. Expect curious stares as you tear off 16 bags at one time, but you'll then be ready to blitz through the fruits and vegetables in just a few minutes. If you have one or two plastic bags left over, you'll know that you forgot an item or two.

When you're back home in your own kitchen, take a moment to consider when or if you'll be going out during the week and will have dinner elsewhere. Then determine generally which night you'll be having each meal. I usually put some of the chicken breasts or meat in the freezer to pull out later in the week, but there's rarely a problem with the fruits and vegetables maintaining their freshness.

Your grocery shopping for the week is now finished. Staple items have been replenished, fresh produce has been put away in the refrigerator, and some of the poultry or beef is tucked safely in the freezer. It's now time to relax and relish the thought of actually ENJOYING cooking for the rest of the week. Remember those three steps in preparing family dinners: planning the meal, grocery shopping, and the actual food preparation? You can officially cross the first two off your "to do" list because they're already completed for the week! You may have to return to the store on Friday to stock up on more fruit or milk, but as far as dinner goes, the stress is over. If your daughter comes home from school wondering what you're cooking that night, don't roll your eyes with a frustrated sigh. Simply let her choose from the various possibilities. You can go off to work without giving the evening meal a moment of thought, or head out late in the afternoon to assist at soccer practice. Even if you arrive home wet and muddy at 5:45 P.M., a warm, home-cooked dinner will be on the table by 6:30 P.M. Make that 6:35 P.M. It could take you five minutes to remove those mud-caked cleats!

Week 1

Chicken Pasta Italiano
with Bread Sticks and Grape Clusters

Marinated Flank Steak
with Fresh Broccoli, Green Salad, and French Bread

Herbed Chicken in Tomato Sauce
with Caesar's Pasta and Fresh Zucchini

Stir Fried Shrimp with Linguini
and Green Salad

Baseball Casserole
and Fruit Salad

A Budding Romance

I know I'm a softie, but there's nothing like hearing daily reports of romance in bloom. When my capable, soft-spoken administrative assistant Sandie McTighe met tall, red-headed Tim on the bus to work, I knew from the first report that this was different. The gorgeous bouquets of flowers that kept appearing on her desk and the little glimmer in her eye were further clues.

Sandie is an accomplished cook, and she and I have shared cooking stories and recipes for years. When her parents came up from Los Angeles for a visit, she and Tim planned a special evening to announce their engagement. Robust and spicy Chicken Pasta Italiano, sprinkled with bacon and dusted with grated Parmesan cheese, was the choice.

2/22/03
Good

Chicken Pasta Italiano
with Bread Sticks and Grape Clusters

SERVES 4

Percentage of
total calories from
the following categories:

Protein: 28%
Carbohydrate: 52%
Fat: 20%

INGREDIENTS

1/2 tsp dry *1/4 tsp dry*

4 boneless, skinned chicken
  breasts
½ pound lean bacon *used turkey or neo + one use Farmertons*
4 large tomatoes
8 cloves garlic
¼ cup chicken broth
2 tablespoons sherry

1½ teaspoons basil, oregano, *1/2 dry*
  thyme, and marjoram *1/4 dry*
⅛ teaspoon crushed red pepper
2 9-ounce packages fresh
  spaghetti *used 8oz dry*
½ cup grated Parmesan cheese

FRUIT SIDE DISH

1 large bunch of grapes

BREAD

8–12 bread sticks

1. For chicken entree, prepare ingredients:
   • Cut chicken breasts in thin slices, then into 1-inch pieces.
   • Cut tomatoes in half and squeeze to remove seeds; chop into
     small chunks.
   • Trim ends and skin from garlic.
2. For fruit, wash grapes and separate into clusters. Place in a
   serving dish.
3. For chicken entree, fill a large pot with water and begin to heat
   for pasta.
4. In a wide frying pan, cook bacon over high heat until crisp.
   Lift out, drain and crumble, then set aside. Discard all but
   2 tablespoons of the drippings.
5. Press garlic and add to the pan along with the chicken. Cook,
   stirring, for about 4 minutes, until chicken is no longer pink.
   Remove chicken pieces from the pan and set aside.
6. Add tomatoes, chicken broth, sherry, basil, oregano, thyme,
   marjoram, and red pepper to pan. Cook for 3 to 4 minutes.
7. Place fresh spaghetti in boiling water and cook about 2 minutes
   until done.
8. Meanwhile, return chicken to tomato mixture, lower heat, and
   stir until heated through.
9. Remove pasta from heat and drain in a large colander. Spoon
   chicken-tomato sauce over individual servings of spaghetti,
   sprinkle with Parmesan cheese, and top with crumbled bacon.
   Serve immediately.

Hint

Take a few minutes
to alphabetize your
spices. If you don't
have a spice rack,
they can lie flat in a
large, shallow drawer
with labels facing up,
or put adhesive
labels on top of the
bottles and stand
them upright in a
deep drawer.

Friends for Life

An hour by car and ferry away from Seattle is a tranquil oasis of hospitality called the Manor Farm Inn in Poulsbo. Sun-splashed white buildings and a profusion of seasonal flowers greet visitors as they wind down the driveway. Cheviot sheep amble slowly across the path and an elegant meal awaits visitors in the cozy dining room. This exquisite inn has been written up in a number of travel magazines and is owned by our dear friend Jill Day. We were neighbors when John and I were first married—John was a medical student, Jill was a special education teacher, and I seemed to be perennially pregnant. Jill was a wonderful cook even then, and one of our favorites was her marinated flank steak. It still is—26 years later.

Marinated Flank Steak
with Fresh Broccoli, Green Salad, and French Bread

SERVES 4

Percentage of total
calories from the
following categories:

Protein: 27%
Carbohydrate: 40%
Fat: 33%

WEEK 1

INGREDIENTS

1½ pound flank steak   green salad

MARINADE

¼ cup soy sauce   1 teaspoon ground ginger
3 tablespoons honey   ½ cup vegetable oil
2 tablespoons vinegar   2 ~~3~~ green onions, sliced
1½ teaspoons garlic powder

VEGETABLE SIDE DISH

1 large bunch of fresh broccoli   salt and pepper
  butter or margarine

GREEN SALAD   BREAD

1 head lettuce or romaine   1 loaf French bread
2 ~~3-4 green onions~~
1 navel orange canned
  salad dressing

Hint

If you make your own vinaigrette salad dressing, remember that mixing the ingredients with a whip for 20 seconds or so will take more bite out of the vinegar than adding the oil and vinegar to the greens individually. For an interesting flavor, substitute fresh lemon or lime juice for the vinegar.

1. For flank steak marinade, mix ingredients, whisking until slightly thickened.
2. Place flank steak in a 9 x 13-inch pan and puncture 5 or 6 times with the tines of a fork to allow marinade to permeate the steak. Pour half of the marinade on the meat, flip to the other side, and repeat. Cover the steak and refrigerate all day or overnight.
3. Turn oven to broil.
4. For vegetable, wash and trim broccoli. Cut into serving-size spears and place in a microwave-proof dish.
5. For flank steak, remove steak from marinade and place on a rimmed cookie sheet or broiler pan. Place in oven on the middle rack, and broil each side for approximately 6 minutes.
6. For green salad, wash and dry lettuce or romaine, then chop and place in a salad bowl. Remove skin from orange and slice sections into small pieces. Slice green onions, including tops, and add to bowl.

continued next page . . .

Marinated Flank Steak

CONTINUED . . .

7. For vegetable, place broccoli in the microwave when it's time to flip the flank steak, and cook on high for 7 to 8 minutes.

8. To complete green salad, add dressing and toss lightly. Serve on individual plates.

9. Remove steak from oven and place on a cutting board to slice.

10. To heat French bread, lower oven heat to 350 degrees. Place bread on a cookie sheet, and put in oven when it has cooled down from broiler setting.

11. To serve flank steak, slice very thinly on the diagonal across the grain. Meat should be slightly pink in the center.

12. To complete vegetable, remove broccoli from microwave. Season with a small amount of butter or margarine, and salt and pepper to taste.

13. Remove French bread and slice.

Advice

FOR ALL AGES

- Whenever possible, go to every game or event your children are involved in.

- "Family Night" can be as fun for older kids as for younger. Through the years the games may progress from Candyland to poker, but the popcorn is still popped and the TV is turned off. Even grown-up kids enjoy participating.

- Try initiating a "Fun 5" minutes of uninterrupted parent/child conversation behind a closed door. If the topic is serious, it becomes a "Terrific 10." Kids call it a lot when they're young . . . Mom and Dad call it a lot when the kids are older.

- Unplug the TV and computer during the week. It's too easy to decide you've studied enough when you can hear a favorite show on in the adjacent room.

- The kitchen table often becomes homework central while Mom—available but not intrusive—cooks dinner. To avoid disruption of important papers and assignments, dinner may need to be served in the dining room, but the pleasant, unexpected result may be far better conversation and quality family time with family members lingering together at the table. Setting the table with linens and candles encourages the enjoyable atmosphere.

- Give your children new calendars for Christmas, with birthdays and phone numbers of family and friends listed on them.

- Bake cookies when your children have friends over. The smell is irresistible and the kids will love to come in the kitchen for warm cookies and conversation.

Beth's Buddy

Dr. Beth Bryant, now a cardiologist in Bowling Green, Kentucky, became our Daughter #3 during her internal medicine residency at Virginia Mason Medical Center in Seattle. Away from her own family, Beth became part of ours and spent a lot of time in our home during her residency years. Her experience as a college basketball player at Auburn University was particularly fascinating to our kids.

Outgoing and vivacious, Beth used to represent Auburn on tours of southern high schools, along with another Auburn athlete whose name is well-known in the sports world: Charles Barkley. It was our pleasure to meet the infamous Charles and some of his then-Philadelphia 76er teammates when they were in Seattle to play the Sonics. Beth kept trying to arrange a "home-cooked meal" for him at our house. Had it ever happened, I would have served this.

Herbed Chicken in Tomato Sauce
with Caesar's Pasta and Fresh Zucchini

SERVES 4

Percentage of total calories from the following categories:

Protein: 25%
Carbohydrate: 40%
Fat: 35%

WEEK 1

INGREDIENTS

8 boneless, skinned chicken breasts
4 tablespoons butter or margarine
8–10 fresh mushrooms
2 cloves garlic

1 8-ounce can tomato sauce
½ teaspoon each basil and oregano
¼ cup light sour cream

CAESAR'S PASTA

2 9-ounce packages fresh angel hair pasta
3 tablespoons light sour cream

3 tablespoons Caesar salad dressing

VEGETABLE SIDE DISH

4 zucchini
butter or margarine

salt and pepper

1. Preheat oven to 375 degrees. Fill a large pot with water and begin to heat for pasta.
2. For chicken entree, arrange 8 individual breasts in a 9 x 13-inch glass baking dish. Melt 3 tablespoons butter and drizzle over chicken. Bake, uncovered, for 10 minutes. Remove from oven and set aside.
3. For vegetable, trim ends off of zucchini and cut in ¼-inch slices. Place slices in a small microwave-proof baking dish.
4. For chicken entree, slice mushrooms and remove skin from garlic.
5. In a saute pan, melt remaining 1 tablespoon butter over medium heat. Add minced garlic and sliced mushrooms and cook for 3 minutes, stirring occasionally. Add tomato sauce, basil, and oregano and simmer for another 3 to 4 minutes. Remove from heat and add light sour cream.
6. For pasta, mix light sour cream and Caesar salad dressing in a small bowl. Set aside.
7. For chicken entree, drain liquid from chicken breasts and spoon tomato-mushroom sauce on top. Return chicken breasts to oven, reduce heat to 350 degrees, and bake for 15 minutes or until done.
8. For vegetable, place zucchini in microwave and cook on high for 7 minutes.
9. For pasta, place fresh pasta in boiling water and cook for 1 to 2 minutes or until done. Remove pasta from heat and drain in a colander. Toss with sauce mixture.
10. To complete vegetable, remove zucchini from microwave and season to taste with a small amount of butter or margarine, salt and pepper.
11. Remove chicken breasts from oven and serve immediately.

Just Do It!

Seattle's Fred Hutchinson Cancer Research Center is a world-class research and treatment facility, and I belong to a fund-raising guild that supports its programs. Our annual event is a 10k run along Lake Washington that raised nearly $100,000 last year. A Shore Run planning meeting was actually an impetus to write this book.

As the meeting ended late one spring afternoon, the conversation turned to dinner plans and the usual complaints about the hassle of daily meal-planning and preparation. It was 5:45 P.M., and no one seemed to know what they were going to prepare for dinner. Some women were heading to the grocery store and another was "going to thaw some hamburger . . ." I could hear the guild president on the phone out in the kitchen saying, "No, that's not right. I said THICK crust and extra cheese."

I sat there feeling guilty, knowing that a package of baby shrimp was in my freezer, and an onion, a green pepper, and a handful of crisp snow peas were in the refrigerator. Tossed together with a little olive oil and spices, this colorful concoction would be spooned over fresh pasta, sprinkled with grated Parmesan and on my family's table in about half an hour. Most important, I wouldn't have spent one minute that day either planning or shopping for it.

It was becoming clear that I needed to publish this book.

Stir Fried Shrimp with Linguini
and Green Salad

SERVES 4

Percentage of total calories from the following categories:

Protein: 27%
Carbohydrate: 38%
Fat: 35%

WEEK 1

INGREDIENTS

½ 1 onion
1 green pepper
½ pound snow peas
2 tablespoons olive oil
¼ teaspoon crushed red pepper
1 teaspoon oregano

1 tablespoon butter or margarine
1 pound cooked baby shrimp
2 9-ounce packages fresh linguini
fresh grated Parmesan cheese

GREEN SALAD

1 head lettuce or romaine
2 3 4 green onions

salad dressing

Hint

Buying spices in bulk saves a lot of money. First time around you need to buy the small bottles, but you can refill with bulk purchases and the labels will already be done.

1. Fill a large pot with water and begin to heat for pasta.
2. For shrimp entree, prepare ingredients:
   - Peel and quarter onion, then slice thinly.
   - Trim green pepper and remove seeds; slice in thin strips.
   - Rinse snow peas and trim ends.
3. For green salad, wash and dry lettuce, then chop and place in a salad bowl. Slice green onions, including tops, and add to salad bowl.
4. For shrimp entree, heat 2 tablespoons olive oil over medium high heat in a large frying pan or wok. When oil is hot, add onion, bell pepper, crushed red pepper, and oregano. Stir fry 3 to 4 minutes or until vegetables are slightly tender. Remove from heat.
5. To complete green salad, add dressing and toss lightly. Serve on individual plates.
6. For shrimp entree, add linguini to boiling water and cook 2 to 3 minutes or until done.
7. Return frying pan to heat and add butter and snow peas. Stir fry just until peas are heated through (about 1 minute). Add shrimp and stir fry until shrimp is heated through (no more than 1 minute). Remove from heat.
8. Remove pasta from heat and drain in a large colander. Serve individual portions of pasta and spoon shrimp and vegetable mixture on top. Sprinkle with Parmesan cheese and serve immediately.

No Relief

Like many young boys, son Brad began playing organized sports at age five. Jill and Julie were still toddlers, but it wasn't long before I wanted the girls to understand that team sports weren't just an activity for big brothers. Deciding my girls needed a role model, I joined a neighborhood women's softball team. John enthusiastically presented me with a baseball mitt for Mother's Day. What else could I say but thank you? I needed it.

Over four seasons, my softball career could be described most accurately as "checkered." There was occasional batting success, but the low point was the night I lost my pitching rhythm and walked (truly!) 17 batters in a row. Our backup pitcher had gone to the symphony that night, and no one else could pitch. I was on my own. That endless inning became a vivid memory to draw upon in later years when my kids needed consolation after their own athletic disappointments.

During that first softball season, I experimented with a simple, hearty rice and chicken casserole that could be made ahead in less than 15 minutes. I put it in the oven as I left for a game, and it would be steaming and ready to serve when I got home. For obvious reasons, we've always referred to it as Baseball Casserole.

Baseball Casserole
and Fruit Salad

SERVES 4

Percentage of total
calories from the
following categories:

Protein: 19%
Carbohydrate: 63%
Fat: 18%

INGREDIENTS

4 boneless, skinned chicken breasts
3 tablespoons butter or margarine
4 cloves garlic
2 cups raw long-grain rice

1 14½-ounce can corn, drained
1 14½-ounce can tomato pieces, with juice
3 cups canned chicken broth

FRUIT SALAD

1–2 bananas
2 oranges

1 apple
grapes

1. Preheat oven to 375 degrees.
2. For casserole, place chicken breasts in a glass baking dish. Bake for 10 minutes.
3. Place butter in a small microwave-proof dish and add pressed garlic. Microwave on high for 40 seconds or until butter is melted.
4. Rinse rice thoroughly and place in a large casserole. Add drained corn, tomatoes and their juice, the butter-garlic mixture, and chicken broth.
5. For fruit salad, prepare and slice fruits and put in a serving dish.
6. For casserole, remove chicken from oven when still slightly pink. Cut into bite-sized chunks and add to casserole dish.
7. Place cover on casserole dish and bake for 45 minutes to an hour, or until rice is done. Serve immediately.

Hint

If you have leftover ripe bananas, peel and freeze them whole to thaw later for banana bread. If you freeze them peeled, you'll have trouble removing the peel later, as the banana will have become mushy as it thaws.

Week 1 Ingredients Lists

Chicken Pasta Italiano with Bread Sticks and Grape Clusters

- ❑ 4 boneless, skinned chicken breasts
- ❑ ½ pound lean bacon
- ❑ 5 ounces grated Parmesan cheese
- ❑ 2 9-ounce packages fresh spaghetti
- ❑ 1 head garlic
- ❑ 4 large tomatoes

- ❑ bread sticks
- ❑ basil
- ❑ chicken bouillon
- ❑ crushed red pepper
- ❑ marjoram
- ❑ oregano
- ❑ sherry
- ❑ thyme
- ❑ 1 bunch grapes

Marinated Flank Steak
with Fresh Broccoli, Green Salad, and French Bread

- ❑ 1½ pound flank steak
- ❑ lettuce or romaine
- ❑ 1 bunch green onions
- ❑ 1 large bunch broccoli
- ❑ 1 orange
- ❑ French bread
- ❑ butter or margarine

- ❑ garlic powder
- ❑ ground ginger
- ❑ honey
- ❑ salad dressing
- ❑ soy sauce
- ❑ vegetable oil
- ❑ vinegar

Herbed Chicken in Tomato Sauce
with Caesar's Pasta and Fresh Zucchini

- ❑ 8 boneless, skinned chicken breasts
- ❑ 2 9-ounce packages fresh angel hair pasta
- ❑ Caesar salad dressing
- ❑ 8-ounce can tomato sauce
- ❑ ½ pint light sour cream

- ❑ 1 head garlic
- ❑ 8–10 mushrooms
- ❑ 4 zucchini

- ❑ basil
- ❑ butter or margarine
- ❑ oregano

Week 1 Ingredients Lists

Stir Fried Shrimp with Linguini and Green Salad

- [ ] 1 pound cooked baby shrimp
- [ ] 2 9-ounce packages fresh linguini
- [ ] 5 ounces grated Parmesan cheese
- [ ] 1 large onion
- [ ] lettuce or romaine
- [ ] 1 bunch green onions

- [ ] 1 green pepper
- [ ] ½ pound snow peas

- [ ] butter or margarine
- [ ] crushed red pepper
- [ ] olive oil
- [ ] oregano
- [ ] salad dressing

Baseball Casserole and Fruit Salad

- [ ] 4 boneless, skinned chicken breasts
- [ ] 16-ounce can corn
- [ ] 14½-ounce can tomato pieces
- [ ] 2 14½-ounce cans chicken broth
- [ ] 1 head garlic

- [ ] 1 bunch grapes
- [ ] 2 oranges
- [ ] 1 small bunch bananas
- [ ] 1 apple

- [ ] butter or margarine
- [ ] raw rice

Week 1 Groceries

- [ ] 1½ pound flank steak
- [ ] ½ pound lean bacon
- [ ] 16 boneless, skinned chicken breasts
- [ ] 1 pound cooked baby shrimp

- [ ] 5 ounces grated Parmesan cheese
- [ ] 2 9-ounce packages fresh spaghetti
- [ ] 2 9-ounce packages fresh linguini
- [ ] 2 9-ounce packages fresh angel hair pasta

- [ ] 1 bottle Caesar salad dressing
- [ ] 1 8-ounce can tomato sauce

- [ ] 1 16-ounce can corn
- [ ] 1 14½-ounce can tomato pieces
- [ ] 2 14½-ounce cans chicken broth
- [ ] ½ pint light sour cream

- [ ] 2 heads garlic
- [ ] 1 large onion
- [ ] 2 heads lettuce or romaine
- [ ] 4 large tomatoes
- [ ] 1 bunch green onions
- [ ] 1 large bunch broccoli
- [ ] 1 green pepper
- [ ] 8–10 mushrooms
- [ ] 4 zucchini
- [ ] ½ pound snow peas
- [ ] 1 large bunch grapes
- [ ] 3 oranges
- [ ] 1 small bunch bananas
- [ ] 1 apple

- [ ] 1 package bread sticks
- [ ] 1 loaf French bread

Check:

- [ ] basil
- [ ] butter/margarine
- [ ] chicken bouillon
- [ ] crushed red pepper
- [ ] garlic powder
- [ ] ground ginger
- [ ] honey
- [ ] marjoram
- [ ] olive oil
- [ ] oregano
- [ ] raw rice
- [ ] salad dressing
- [ ] salt and fresh ground black pepper
- [ ] sherry
- [ ] soy sauce
- [ ] thyme
- [ ] vegetable oil
- [ ] vinegar

Week 2

Chicken Dijon with Angel Hair Pasta ✳
and Fresh Zucchini

Chili ✳
with Honeydew Melon Slices and French Bread

Fish Fettuccine
and Green Salad

Fried Rice ✳
and Fruit Salad

Beef and Vegetable Stir Fry ✳
with Rice and Fresh Orange Slices

Variation on the Same Theme

On the shore of Lake Washington is the tiny neighborhood of Madison Park, a quaint mix of older homes, restaurants, and shops. Young professionals in sweats push strollers and are on a first-name basis with well-heeled matrons. The aroma of espresso fills the air in the congenial warmth of Tully's, where businessmen and joggers sit side-by-side. Another favorite place for breakfast or lunch is the cozy Madison Park Café, operated by my good friend and frequent tennis partner, Peggy Stamm.

A few years ago Peggy shared with me her version of Chicken Dijon, using plump boneless breasts of chicken sauced in a mustardy mix of artichoke hearts, sweet onions, and mushrooms with a splash of white wine. One evening I prepared the entree for my family. Back for seconds, son Brad commented that it would be even better if the chicken breasts were cut in small pieces and served over angel hair pasta. I tried it that way the next time, adding a small amount of light sour cream to make a smooth sauce. We all agreed he was right.

Chicken Dijon with Angel Hair Pasta
and Fresh Zucchini

Percentage of total calories from the following categories:

Protein: 26%
Carbohydrate: 43%
Fat: 31%

WEEK 2

INGREDIENTS

4 boneless, skinned chicken breasts	3 cloves garlic
½ 1 large sweet onion	1 tablespoon Dijon mustard
8 mushrooms	⅓ cup white wine
1 6-ounce jar marinated artichoke hearts	½ cup light sour cream
2 tablespoons butter or margarine	2 9-ounce packages fresh angel hair pasta

VEGETABLE SIDE DISH

3–4 medium zucchini	salt and pepper to taste
1 tablespoon butter or margarine	

1. Fill a large pot with water and begin to heat for pasta.
2. For chicken entree, prepare ingredients:
   - Cut chicken breasts into ¾-inch chunks.
   - Peel and quarter onion, then slice thinly.
   - Trim stems off of mushrooms and slice thinly.
   - Drain artichoke hearts and cut into small pieces.
3. For vegetable, trim zucchini and cut into ¼-inch slices. Place in a microwave-proof pan and set aside.
4. For chicken entree, place 2 tablespoons butter in a wide frying pan or wok over medium high heat. Press garlic and add. Add chicken pieces and cook for 1 to 2 minutes.
5. For vegetable, microwave zucchini on high for 6 minutes.
6. For chicken entree, add onion slices to chicken and cook 1 minute more. Add mushroom slices and artichoke pieces. Continue cooking until chicken pieces are no longer pink (approximately 4 minutes) and remove pan from heat. Reduce burner temperature to low.
7. Put pasta in boiling water and cook 1 to 2 minutes or until done.
8. Add Dijon mustard and wine to chicken mixture and stir carefully. Place pan back on burner and add light sour cream. Stir gently until sauce forms. Remove from heat.
9. To complete vegetable, remove zucchini from microwave. Season lightly with small amount of butter, salt, and pepper.
10. For chicken entree, drain pasta in a large colander.
11. Spoon Chicken Dijon over pasta and serve immediately, accompanied by fresh zucchini.

Hint

A serrated knife blade is an easy way to lift long strands of cooking pasta out of the boiling water to test for doneness. The blade's notches stop the strands from sliding back into the bubbling water.

It Takes All Kinds

Grandmas come in all shapes and sizes. John's mother is the classic variety whose 14 devoted grandchildren have spent countless hours baking cookies and making crafts at her comfortable home on the hill.

My mother is best described as a millennium grandma: she won't reveal her age, is more up on the latest trends than I am, and would much rather play golf than bake cookies. This is her chili recipe. Maybe it's what keeps her young.

Chili
with Honeydew Melon Slices and French Bread

SERVES 4

Percentage of total
calories from the
following categories:

INGREDIENTS

½ 1 onion
1 tablespoon oil
1 pound leanest ground beef
3 cups regular strength beef
   broth
1 10¾-ounce can tomato puree
1 14½-ounce can tomato pieces
1 15½-ounce can kidney beans,
   drained

1 15½-ounce can corn, drained
½ teaspoon each cumin and
   oregano
   salt and pepper to taste
¼–½ cup grated Cheddar cheese
   light sour cream

Protein: 19%
Carbohydrate: 53%
Fat: 28%

WEEK 2

Hint

Use a melon-baller to
remove the seeds or
core from all sorts
of fruits and
vegetables like
melons, apples,
pears, zucchini, etc.
This method is quick,
easy, and preserves
more of the fruit or
vegetable.

FRUIT SIDE DISH	BREAD
1 honeydew melon	1 loaf French bread

1. For chili, peel and quarter onion, then slice thinly.
2. Place oil in a large stockpot or Dutch oven over medium-high heat. Crumble beef into pot, add onion, and cook, stirring occasionally, until the meat is no longer pink and the onion is soft; drain and discard fat.
3. Reduce heat and stir in beef broth, tomato puree, tomato pieces, kidney beans, corn, and spices. Simmer for at least half an hour over low heat.
4. Preheat oven to 350 degrees.
5. Place French bread on a cookie sheet and heat in warm oven.
6. For fruit, peel and slice honeydew melon into wedges. Place in a serving bowl.
7. For chili, grate Cheddar cheese. To serve chili, spoon into individual bowls, top with a dollop of light sour cream, and sprinkle with grated Cheddar cheese.
8. Slice French bread.

To Russia with Love

In 1986, daughter Jill was one of twelve American students chosen to attend Moscow School #20 for five weeks. The political situation was different back then, and we felt some anxiety watching the huge SAS jet, with our young daughter on board, lumber down the runway headed for Copenhagen and then Moscow. As it turned out, the American students were warmly welcomed, and they shared unforgettable moments of goodwill and friendship with their Russian hosts. Jill bought a watercolor of St. Basil's Cathedral from an underground artist and traded a pair of her own jeans for a Russian Army officer's cap, toured Red Square, and was awed by timeless Leningrad. Language was a constant challenge, and her letters grumbled a little about the starchy, high-fat Russian food and the scarcity of fresh fruits and vegetables. But Russian ice cream— rich cubes served on sticks by street vendors— aaahh! When Jill arrived home five weeks later, she was very ready for a healthy, home-cooked meal. Because she hadn't had seafood for five weeks, her first request was this entree.

Fish Fettuccine
and Green Salad

INGREDIENTS

1 onion
1 28-ounce can Italian-style
   tomatoes, drained
½ cup parsley
⅔ to ¾ pound white fish fillets
   (halibut or cod)
or other meat

2 tablespoons olive oil
½ teaspoon basil
   salt and pepper to taste
2 9-ounce packages fresh
   fettuccine

GREEN SALAD

1 head lettuce or romaine
3–4 green onions

1 orange *can*
   salad dressing

1. For seafood entree, prepare ingredients:
   - Peel and quarter onion, then slice very thinly.
   - Drain tomatoes and slice in rings.
   - Chop parsley.
   - Check fish fillets for bones and cut into 1-inch cubes.
2. Fill a large pot with water and begin to heat for pasta.
3. For green salad, wash and dry lettuce, then chop and place in a salad bowl. Slice green onions, including tops, and add to salad bowl.
4. For seafood entree, place oil in a wide frying pan or wok over medium-high heat. Add onion and saute until limp. Add chopped tomatoes, parsley, basil, salt, and pepper. Reduce heat and simmer, uncovered, for 5 minutes.
5. For green salad, peel orange and cut sections into bite-sized pieces, then add to salad bowl.
6. For seafood entree, add fish to saucepan and cook approximately 5 minutes, occasionally turning fish gently until it is opaque.
7. To complete green salad, add dressing and toss lightly. Serve on individual plates.
8. For seafood entree, place fettuccine in boiling water. Cook 2 to 3 minutes or until done. Remove pasta from heat and drain in a large colander.
9. Spoon tomato and fish sauce over individual servings of fettuccine. Serve immediately.

SERVES 4

Percentage of total
calories from the
following categories:

Protein: 22%
Carbohydrate: 46%
Fat: 32%

WEEK 2

Hint
If you never know exactly how many you're going to be feeding, keep extra cans of Italian-style tomatoes on hand to stretch this and other entrees.

Not to Worry, Mom

One of our most memorable family trips was our first ski adventure, to Snowmass in Colorado. Our friend Gail Ransom's father, Robert Ingersoll, United States ambassador to Japan from 1970 to 1972, owns a spacious home secluded in the woods, walking distance from the snowy slopes of Green Cabin. Thirteen of us, including seven children between the ages of four and eight, descended on the house one March.

Keeping socks dry and mouths fed was a logistical challenge for the adults, but more important were the lessons in independence our children faced. Skiing provides frequent opportunities to boost a child's self-confidence if you can loosen the reins and let them struggle a bit, even when your instincts are more protective. An example from that trip comes to mind.

On our first afternoon at Snowmass I went to pick up daughter Julie from the Kinderheim Day Care and was told that she was out skiing on Fanny Hill. Four-year-old Julie had never been on a chairlift before. Anxious and concerned, I rushed over in time to see her swoosh down off the chairlift with a wide, confident grin. Not wanting to overreact, I calmly asked her if the teacher had gone along the first time she rode the chair. Julie shook her head no, and then in a reassuring tone explained, "But it was OK, Mom. I was with Hillary … and she's five."

That week our dinners for thirteen needed to be quick, hearty, and inexpensive. Just like this Fried Rice.

Fried Rice
and Fruit Salad

INGREDIENTS

3 cups raw rice
3 eggs, plus 1 egg white
1½ cups cut-up cooked ham, turkey, or turkey ham

6–8 green onions
3 tablespoons oil
light soy sauce

FRUIT SALAD

1 small bunch grapes
1 banana

1 apple
2 oranges

1. For fried rice, cook rice according to package directions.
2. Prepare ingredients:
   - Break eggs and egg white into a small bowl and beat lightly.
   - Cut ham and turkey into ⅜-inch cubes.
   - Slice green onions, including tops.
3. For fruit salad, prepare fruits and place in a serving bowl. Set aside.
4. For fried rice, heat 1 teaspoon oil in a wok over medium-high heat. Pour in half of the beaten eggs and cook briefly until egg "pancake" begins to solidify. Lift up edges and let beaten egg seep under. When the pancake begins to brown, flip it and briefly cook the other side. Remove and repeat the process with the remaining beaten egg. Set cooked egg pancakes aside.
5. Add 1 tablespoon oil to the wok and stir fry ham or turkey and green onion together for 1 to 2 minutes or until heated through.
6. Add remaining oil and transfer steamed rice to the wok. Fold carefully so that turkey ham is well distributed.
7. Chop egg pancakes and add to rice.
8. Add light soy to taste and toss gently.
9. Remove from heat and serve immediately.

WEEK 2

Hint

You can wash grapes, strawberries, mushrooms, green beans, etc., without removing them from the plastic bag. Fill the plastic bag with cool water and slosh the fruits or vegetables around, then poke a hole in the bottom of the bag to drain out the water.

I Want to Be Like Mia

Most women my age didn't play team sports when they were growing up. We played a little baseball with the boys until they joined Little League. Then we had to put away our mitts. We played some basketball, but had to choose offense OR defense, could only dribble three times, and never, ever crossed the centerline.

But women have now learned that athletics mean a whole lot more than mud, sweat, and beers. Sports enhance life. Extra energy, stress reduction, and a more positive self-image result from any athletic endeavor. Equally important, camaraderie and friendship are the pleasant by-products of team participation.

I've endured some teasing for the seven years I played women's soccer. It's a rough, physical sport, and I'm not very solid and am fairly easily intimidated. But I wouldn't trade those nights running around on a sloppy turf field in the cold Northwest rain for anything. We all get a boost from doing something out of our comfort zone. Fair of failure should never keep us from trying new experiences.

So what could soccer possibly have to do with a stir fry? The simplicity of this entree made it something the kids managed easily on their own, those nights that I was off giving it my all at left wing.

Beef and Vegetable Stir Fry
with Rice and Fresh Orange Slices

SERVES 4

Percentage of total
calories from the
following categories:

Protein: 19%
Carbohydrate: 53%
Fat: 27%

WEEK 2

INGREDIENTS

3 cups raw rice cooked with
    4 cups water
1 pound sirloin, trimmed
1 large onion

2 carrots
1 small red bell pepper
1 bunch broccoli
2 tablespoons oil

MARINADE

1 tablespoon vegetable oil
1 tablespoon soy sauce
1 tablespoon ketchup

1 tablespoon sherry
1 tablespoon cornstarch
1 tablespoon sesame oil

FRUIT SIDE DISH

3 large navel oranges

1. For beef entree, cook rice according to package directions.
2. Mix marinade ingredients in a medium bowl.
3. Slice sirloin into ¼-inch strips and cut strips into 1-inch pieces. Place in marinade and stir to coat meat.
4. Prepare vegetables:
   - Peel and quarter onion, then slice thinly.
   - Peel and slice carrots on a diagonal.
   - Slice red pepper into thin strips.
   - Trim stalks off broccoli and cut in small flowerets.
5. Place broccoli in a microwave-proof dish and cook on high for 4 minutes.
6. For fruit, cut both ends off of an orange with a sharp knife. Stand orange upright on a cutting board and, starting at the top, slice down and around the sides just under the skin, until all skin is removed. Turn orange on its side and cut in ¼- to ½-inch slices, then place on a serving dish. Repeat. Slices will look like pinwheels.
7. For beef entree, heat 1 tablespoon oil over medium-high heat in a wok or large frying pan. Add onion and stir fry for 1 to 2 minutes. Add carrot and stir fry another 1 to 2 minutes. Add red pepper and partially-cooked broccoli. Stir fry 1 minute. Remove vegetables and place in a bowl.
8. Add sirloin to pan and cook for 2 minutes or until meat is still slightly pink. Remove from heat and add vegetables, stirring until sauce forms.
9. Serve beef and vegetable mixture over rice.

Hint

If you have leftovers, freeze cut-up bits of the beef, vegetables, and rice to later make a hearty soup for lunch.

Week 2 Ingredients Lists

Chicken Dijon with Angel Hair Pasta and Fresh Zucchini

- [ ] 4 boneless, skinned chicken breasts
- [ ] 2 9-ounce packages angel hair pasta
- [ ] 6-ounce jar marinated artichoke hearts
- [ ] 1 head garlic
- [ ] 1 large sweet onion

- [ ] ½ pint light sour cream
- [ ] 8 mushrooms
- [ ] 3–4 medium zucchini

- [ ] butter or margarine
- [ ] Dijon mustard
- [ ] white wine

Chili with Honeydew Melon Slices and French Bread

- [ ] 1 pound leanest ground beef
- [ ] 1 14½-ounce can tomato pieces
- [ ] 1 10¾-ounce can tomato puree
- [ ] 1 15½-ounce can corn
- [ ] 1 15½-ounce can dark red kidney beans
- [ ] 2 14½-ounce cans beef broth
- [ ] 4 ounces Cheddar cheese

- [ ] ½ pint light sour cream
- [ ] 1 large onion
- [ ] 1 honeydew melon
- [ ] French bread

- [ ] cumin
- [ ] oregano
- [ ] vegetable oil

Fish Fettuccine and Green Salad

- [ ] ⅔–¾ pound halibut or cod fillets
- [ ] 2 9-ounce packages fresh fettucine
- [ ] 1 28-ounce can Italian-style tomatoes
- [ ] 1 large onion
- [ ] 1 bunch green onions

- [ ] lettuce or romaine
- [ ] parsley
- [ ] 1 orange

- [ ] basil
- [ ] olive oil
- [ ] salad dressing

Week 2 Ingredients Lists

Fried Rice and Fruit Salad

- [ ] ½ pound ham, cooked turkey, or turkey ham
- [ ] 1 bunch green onions
- [ ] 2 oranges
- [ ] 1 small bunch grapes
- [ ] 1 small bunch bananas
- [ ] 1 green apple
- [ ] 4 eggs
- [ ] light soy sauce
- [ ] raw rice
- [ ] vegetable oil

Beef and Vegetable Stir Fry with Rice and Fresh Orange Slices

- [ ] 1 pound sirloin steak
- [ ] 1 large onion
- [ ] 1 small red bell pepper
- [ ] 1 bunch broccoli
- [ ] 2 carrots
- [ ] 3 oranges
- [ ] cornstarch
- [ ] ketchup
- [ ] raw rice
- [ ] sesame oil
- [ ] sherry
- [ ] soy sauce
- [ ] vegetable oil

Week 2 Groceries

- [ ] 1   pound leanest ground beef
- [ ] 1   pound sirloin steak
- [ ] ½   pound ham, cooked turkey, or turkey ham
- [ ] 4   boneless, skinned chicken breasts
- [ ] ⅔–¾   pound halibut or cod fillets

- [ ] 2   9-ounce packages fresh fettuccine
- [ ] 2   9-ounce packages angel hair pasta

- [ ] 1   28-ounce can Italian-style tomatoes
- [ ] 1   14½-ounce can tomato pieces
- [ ] 1   10¾-ounce can tomato puree
- [ ] 1   15½-ounce can corn
- [ ] 1   6-ounce jar marinated artichoke hearts
- [ ] 1   15½-ounce can dark red kidney beans
- [ ] 2   14½-ounce cans beef broth

- [ ] 4   ounces Cheddar cheese
- [ ] ½   pint light sour cream

- [ ] 1   head garlic
- [ ] 4   large sweet onions
- [ ] 1   head lettuce or romaine
- [ ] 1   large bunch green onions
- [ ] 1   bunch parsley
- [ ] 8   mushrooms
- [ ] 1   small red bell pepper
- [ ] 3–4   medium zucchini
- [ ] 1   bunch broccoli
- [ ] 2   carrots
- [ ] 1   honeydew melon
- [ ] 6   oranges
- [ ] 1   small bunch grapes
- [ ] 1   small bunch bananas
- [ ] 1   green apple

- [ ] 1   loaf French bread

Check:

- [ ] basil
- [ ] butter/margarine
- [ ] cornstarch
- [ ] cumin
- [ ] Dijon mustard
- [ ] eggs
- [ ] ketchup
- [ ] light soy sauce
- [ ] olive oil
- [ ] oregano
- [ ] raw rice
- [ ] salad dressing
- [ ] salt and fresh ground black pepper
- [ ] sesame oil
- [ ] sherry
- [ ] soy sauce
- [ ] vegetable oil
- [ ] white wine

Week 3

Teriyaki Chicken
with Cilantro Rice Pilaf and Snow Peas

Beef Fajitas Stir Fry
with Melon Slices

Lemon Mushroom Sole
with Fresh Broccoli and French Bread

Dollie's Chicken
with Stir Fried Vegetables
and Parmesan Baked Potato Slices

Italian Spaghetti
with Green Salad and Focaccia

Alive and Kicking

John did an internal medicine residency at the Mayo Clinic in Rochester, Minnesota, back in the early '70s. It was a demanding time for a young family like ours but we remember those years fondly. Thanksgiving and Christmas were spent with friends rather than family. We had little money and even less free time, but everyone we knew was enduring the same financial constraints and demanding call schedules. Out of our shared experiences grew a real camaraderie.

Our closest friends in Rochester were Jim Johnston, now a gastroenterologist back home in Mississippi, and his wife, Elta. A genteel Southerner, Elta's sharp wit and intellect nevertheless found humor in any situation, particularly our infamous lobster dinner. She had invited us over for an elegant meal (rare for all of us!) and had purchased four live Maine lobsters to serve. Unfortunately, the heating element in the large electric pot she rented to cook them in was faulty, and we ended up with four very alive lobsters thrashing and splashing in little individual saucepans on top of her stove.

How times have changed. Elta, who used to take their sheepdog Ralph for a walk and consider it major exercise, recently ran a marathon and teaches college English. On their last visit to Seattle, we shared the following meal.

Teriyaki Chicken
with Cilantro Rice Pilaf and Snow Peas

SERVES 4

Percentage of total
calories from the
following categories:

Protein: 25%
Carbohydrate: 56%
Fat: 19%

INGREDIENTS

10–12 boneless, skinned chicken thighs   ¼ cup toasted sesame seeds

MARINADE

⅔ cup firmly packed brown sugar   2 cloves garlic
⅓ cup soy sauce   2 teaspoons sesame oil

RICE PILAF

4 cups chicken broth   2 stalks celery
3 tablespoons butter or margarine   ½ bunch cilantro
2 cups raw rice   6–8 green onions
2 medium carrots   ½ cup slivered almonds

VEGETABLE SIDE DISH

1 pound snow peas

1. For chicken marinade, combine brown sugar, soy sauce, pressed garlic, and sesame oil in a large saucepan. Cook over medium heat until syrupy and remove from heat. Place chicken thighs in marinade and mix with a spoon so that all pieces are coated. Refrigerate until ready to broil.
2. For rice pilaf, preheat oven to 350 degrees. Pour chicken broth into a large casserole dish and place it in the oven.
3. Melt butter in a large, flat saucepan or frying pan over medium-high heat. Rinse rice, place in pan, and stir until rice is lightly browned.
4. Coarsely chop peeled and trimmed carrots, celery, cilantro, and green onions. A food processor works very well for this.
5. Remove casserole dish from oven and carefully spoon browned rice into hot chicken broth. Cover casserole and place in oven. Bake 25 minutes.
6. For vegetable, prepare snow peas while the rice pilaf bakes. Wash, trim ends, and place snow peas in a microwave.
7. Remove rice pilaf from oven after 25 minutes and mix in coarsely chopped vegetables and slivered almonds. Return to oven and bake another 20 minutes.

Continued next page . . .

Hint

Kitchen clean-up is a breeze if you do the pots and pans as you go along. Or, if time is short and you have a double sink, fill the second sink with soapy water and keep putting your dirty prep bowls and utensils in there to soak. The dirty dishes are hidden under the bubbles until after dinner and your kitchen looks neat and clean as you cook.

Note: If possible, prepare the marinade the previous night, or early in the morning. The chicken is most flavorful if it marinates at least 8 hours.

WEEK 3

8. To broil chicken, remove rice pilaf from oven and turn oven to broil. (Pilaf will stay warm covered.) Place chicken thighs upside-down on a foil-covered broiler pan on the middle rack of the oven. Broil 8 to 9 minutes, remove pan, and turn thighs over. Broil 4 minutes, remove, and sprinkle with toasted sesame seeds. Return to oven and broil 4 minutes more or until done.

9. To complete vegetable, place snow peas in microwave on high for 3½ minutes. Serve immediately.

FOR TEENAGERS

- When planning a trip, especially to a foreign country, fill a large manila envelope with your research on a city, then let your teenager sort through the information and be the "tour guide" in that destination, managing the finances, keeping a budget, and recording expenses. They remain enthusiastic and interested.

- Teenagers love having a "Seven-11" drawer in the kitchen, filled with snacks like microwave popcorn, granola bars, crackers, raisins, homemade cookies, hot chocolate—things teenagers enjoy between school and athletic practices and activities.

- Try the "Same Day Rule" to enforce a midnight curfew for your teenager. You must come home the same day you leave! It's hard to misinterpret.

- A great way to deal with the teenager who wails, "Why can't I go/wear/do _____? EVERYBODY's going/wearing/doing it!" is to first figure out how popular the trend is and then ask the child to "name two" or "name ten." If the child can, then give the request some serious thought. If not, the request will usually vanish.

- Remember that not everything has to be done your way. Pick your battles with teenagers.

- The written word is powerful. Write letters to your teenagers to express your frustration . . . kids tend to reread what you say. Use Post-it love notes on pillows and in jacket pockets and duffel bags—reminders of how much you care about them.

Just Call Me "June"

Daughter Julie's good friend Adam Hamilton was a fixture in our home for nearly three years. This self-described "King of Bland" generally preferred a plain bowl of rice to a more adventurous entree, but he always gamely sampled whatever I prepared. Adam was the first up for seconds, however, the night these fajitas were served, and I'll never forget his comment. In his best Eddie Haskell voice, Adam declared, "You really outdid yourself this time, Mrs. K!"

Beef Fajitas Stir Fry
with Melon Slices

SERVES 4

Percentage of total
calories from the
following categories:

Protein: 24%
Carbohydrate: 44%
Fat: 32%

INGREDIENTS

1¼ pound sirloin steak	1 teaspoon cumin
1 large onion	¼ teaspoon salt
1 red bell pepper	2 teaspoons cornstarch
3 green chiles	2 tablespoons vegetable oil
3 medium-sized Roma tomatoes	cilantro sprigs
large avocado	light sour cream
3 cloves garlic	10 8-inch flour tortillas
¼ cup lime juice	

FRUIT SIDE DISH

1 honeydew melon

Hint

If your sirloin steak
is frozen, only thaw
it partially before
slicing for fajitas—
it will be much easier
to slice.

WEEK 3

1. For fajitas, prepare ingredients:
   - Slice sirloin in ¼-inch slices, then into 1-inch pieces.
   - Peel and quarter onion, then slice thinly.
   - Trim red pepper and slice in thin strips.
   - Dice green chiles (use ¼ to ⅓ cup depending on your taste).
   - Trim stem end of Roma tomatoes and cut in quarters. Using your thumb, remove seeds and cut in ¼-inch slices.
   - Pit, peel, and dice avocado.
   - Squeeze fresh lime juice.
2. For fruit, remove rind from honeydew melon, slice in wedges, and place in a serving dish.
3. For fajitas, place fresh lime juice in a bowl and mix in cumin, salt, and cornstarch.
4. Heat 1 tablespoon oil in a wok. Add meat and stir fry over medium-high heat until lightly browned, but still pink. With a slotted spoon, transfer meat to a bowl and pour out remaining juice.
5. Add 1 tablespoon oil to wok, then onion slices and pressed garlic. Stir fry for 1 to 2 minutes and add red pepper and chiles. Stir fry for approximately 3 more minutes until onion is slightly soft.
6. Pierce tortilla package to allow steam to escape and place in microwave. Heat tortillas on high for approximately 1½ minutes.
7. Add lime juice mixture to vegetables, along with drained sirloin and tomato slices. Cook, stirring, until liquid comes to a light boil. Season with salt and pepper.
8. Spoon beef and vegetables into warm tortillas. Add a sprig of cilantro, avocado chunks, and a dollop of light sour cream to taste. Serve immediately.

Words to the Wise

In 1996, Jill and Justin were married by Dr. Dale Turner, who wove humanity, eloquence, simplicity, warmth, inspiration, and humor into every one of his Sunday sermons for 24 years at Seattle's University Congregational Church. Now in his 80s and retired, Dr. Turner still reaches Northwest residents through a weekly newspaper column.

In his book *Different Seasons*, Dr. Turner gives purpose to the simple acts of daily living many of us sometimes see as menial.

One may desire to accomplish great and noble tasks, but the big souls are those who tackle humble tasks as though they were great and noble. Most of us do not have the potential to make such a phenomenal contribution to life, but it is heartening to know that faithfulness in offering even the smallest of gifts can be of value— a letter, a call, a kind word, a listening ear, a gift to a needy cause— such little acts of love and faithfulness make ours a better world.

Or, in the most simple terms, "The smallest good deed is better than the grandest good intention." How true!

Lemon Mushroom Sole
with Fresh Broccoli and French Bread

SERVES 4

Percentage of total
calories from the
following categories:

Protein: 49%
Carbohydrate: 24%
Fat: 27%

INGREDIENTS

12 fresh mushrooms
½ cup chopped parsley
2 tablespoons lemon juice
2 tablespoons butter or margarine
1 tablespoon flour
1 cup whipping cream

1 tablespoon sherry
2 pounds sole fillets
1 tablespoon grated Parmesan
  cheese
1 tablespoon bread crumbs
  salt and pepper to taste

VEGETABLE SIDE DISH

1 large bunch fresh broccoli   butter or margarine

BREAD

1 loaf French bread

1. Preheat oven to 400 degrees.
2. For sole, prepare ingredients:
   - Wash mushrooms carefully, trim, and slice.
   - Chop parsley.
   - Squeeze fresh lemon juice.
3. For vegetable, trim broccoli and cut stalks in serving size pieces. Place in a microwave-proof dish.
4. For sole, melt butter with lemon juice in a heavy saucepan. Add mushrooms and saute over low heat for 10 minutes, stirring occasionally. Blend in flour, gradually add cream, and simmer, stirring until thickened. Simmer 10 minutes longer, stirring occasionally. Add sherry, salt, and pepper to taste.
5. Place fillets in a large shallow baking dish; sprinkle with parsley. Pour mushroom sauce over fish, sprinkle with Parmesan cheese and bread crumbs.
6. Place baking dish in oven for 10 to 12 minutes or until fish flakes easily.
7. To complete vegetable, place broccoli in microwave and cook on high for 7 to 8 minutes. When tender crisp, season lightly with butter or margarine, salt, and pepper.
8. Place French bread on a cookie sheet and heat in warm oven. Bake 5 minutes or until golden brown. Slice and serve immediately.

Hint

To always have fresh bread, keep it in the freezer. It takes just a second to thaw out naturally, and toast can be made just as quickly with frozen as with fresh bread.

WEEK 3

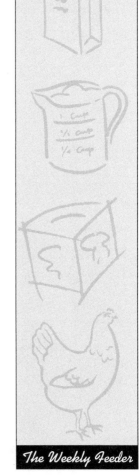

Caught in the Act

For many years John and I enjoyed an annual August trip to Salishan Resort on the Oregon Coast, with a group of close friends who included Hugh and Dollie Armstrong, the parents of '84 Olympic giant slalom gold medalist Debbie Armstrong. There were campfires on the beach and sandy sing-alongs, but the real highlight was an event we dubbed (often literally) "Midnight Golf." Necessary equipment included an ancient wood-shafted golf club, a bucket of battered practice balls, a camping flashlight, and a water hazard some 150 yards in the distance. Twelve of us huddled silently as, one by one, we teed up an old ball and tried to reach the water hazard using the antique wood. Muffling our laughter was difficult, but necessary. The only way to tell if a shot hit the mark was to hear the distant plunk as it landed in the water. We even divided into teams and kept score.

It was an amusing annual escapade until one year when the resort's security patrol drove out onto the course to see what was going on. Funny, they didn't see the humor in our friendly competition.

Dollie Armstrong is best known for her wonderful home-baked wheat bread and jams, but one night she was improvising dinner and stir fried a delightful combination of vegetables. I thought how nice those vegetables would be served over chicken breasts baked gently in the oven with butter and lots of fresh garlic. Back in Seattle, I tried the following entree.

Dollie's Chicken
with Stir Fried Vegetables and Parmesan Baked Potato Slices

SERVES 4

Percentage of total calories from the following categories:

Protein: 24%
Carbohydrate: 39%
Fat: 34%

INGREDIENTS

2 tablespoons butter or margarine	8 boneless, skinned chicken breasts
4 cloves garlic	

STIR FRIED VEGETABLES

½ 1 onion	10 cherry tomatoes
3 carrots	1 cup bean sprouts
1 zucchini	1 tablespoon vegetable oil

POTATO SIDE DISH

4 baking potatoes	salt and pepper
1–2 tablespoons butter or margarine	¼ cup grated Parmesan cheese

Hint

Vegetable peelings can be added to your "worm farm" to make excellent compost for container flowers.

WEEK 3

1. For potatoes, heat oven to 350 degrees. Wash potatoes and, leaving skins on, slice in ¼-inch slices. Place butter on a rimmed cookie sheet (you may need two cookie sheets if potatoes are large) and put into oven briefly until butter melts. Spread melted butter over the surface of the cookie sheet.
2. Fill cookie sheet with flat potato slices. Salt and pepper to taste, then sprinkle with Parmesan cheese. Place in oven and bake 45 minutes or until golden brown and crispy.
3. For chicken, place 2 tablespoons butter in a small glass dish and add pressed garlic. Microwave on high 1 minute or until butter melts.
4. Prepare stir fried vegetables:
   - Peel and quarter onion, then slice thinly.
   - Peel carrots and slice thinly on the diagonal.
   - Trim zucchini; cut in ¼-inch slices.
   - Cut cherry tomatoes in half.
5. For chicken, place breasts in a large shallow baking dish. Drizzle with butter/garlic mixture. Bake 20 minutes or until no longer pink.
6. To complete the stir fried vegetables, allow a total of 10 minutes. Add oil to a wok or wide frying pan over medium-high heat. Add onion and stir fry 2 to 3 minutes. Add carrot and stir fry 2 to 3 minutes. Add zucchini and stir fry 1 to 2 minutes. Remove vegetables from heat until chicken and potatoes are done, then carefully toss in cherry tomatoes and sprouts and warm briefly until heated through.
7. To serve chicken, place 1 or 2 chicken breasts on a plate and spoon vegetable mix on top. Accompany with potato slices and serve immediately.

Cartoons and the Y Chromosome

When Brad was a junior in high school, his basketball team placed second in the state AA high school tournament. Throughout the season, players took turns hosting a team dinner in their homes before important games. It was always fun, but there was subtle pressure. Although the boys claimed not to be superstitious, the team never returned if they lost the game after a meal at your home.

When our girls got to high school, we learned that the tradition was the same before their soccer and basketball games. It was fascinating to contrast the differences in male-female pre-game habits: the girls ate very little and spent their extra time doing homework. The boys sat around eating huge quantities of pasta and bread and watched cartoons. I never understood how those empty heads and full stomachs could focus on the game, but they certainly proved me wrong. This easy spaghetti was a favorite with all the teams, male and female.

Italian Spaghetti

with Green Salad and Focaccia

SERVES 4

Percentage of total calories from the following categories:

Protein: 25%
Carbohydrate: 45%
Fat: 30%

INGREDIENTS

1 tablespoon oil	2 9-ounce packages fresh
1 pound lean ground beef	spaghetti
1 26-ounce jar spaghetti sauce	grated Parmesan cheese

GREEN SALAD

1 head lettuce or romaine   salad dressing
2 3-4 green onions

BREAD

1 loaf focaccia bread   1 tablespoon olive oil

1. For entree, heat oil in a wide frying pan over medium-high heat and add ground beef. Cook until no longer pink and drain.
2. Fill a large pot with water and begin to heat for pasta.
3. Add spaghetti sauce to ground beef and heat until bubbly.
4. For focaccia, heat oven to 350 degrees. Brush bread with olive oil and sprinkle lightly with Parmesan cheese, if desired.
5. For green salad, wash and dry lettuce, then chop and place in a salad bowl. Slice green onions, including tops, and add to salad bowl.
6. Place focaccia loaf on a cookie sheet and heat in warm oven until golden brown.
7. To complete green salad, add dressing and toss lightly. Serve on individual plates.
8. For entree, place fresh spaghetti in boiling water and cook 2 to 3 minutes or until done.
9. Remove spaghetti from heat and drain in a large colander. Serve with spaghetti sauce sprinkled with Parmesan cheese.
10. Slice focaccia into 8 wedges and serve immediately.

WEEK 3

Hint

Here's a sure-fire way to open tight lids on glass jars—tap the lid three times on the counter, wait two seconds and tap three more times. Works every time!

Week 3 Ingredients Lists

Teriyaki Chicken with Cilantro Rice Pilaf and Snow Peas

- ❑ 10–12 boneless, skinned chicken thighs
- ❑ 3 14½-ounce cans chicken broth
- ❑ 3-ounce package slivered almonds
- ❑ 1 head garlic
- ❑ 1 bunch green onions
- ❑ cilantro
- ❑ 1 pound snow peas

- ❑ 2 medium carrots
- ❑ 1 small bunch celery

- ❑ brown sugar
- ❑ butter or margarine
- ❑ raw rice
- ❑ sesame oil
- ❑ soy sauce
- ❑ toasted sesame seeds

Beef Fajitas Stir Fry with Melon Slices

- ❑ 1¼-pound sirloin steak
- ❑ 10 8-inch flour tortillas
- ❑ small can green chiles
- ❑ ½ pint light sour cream
- ❑ 1 head garlic
- ❑ 1 large onion
- ❑ 3 medium Roma tomatoes
- ❑ 1 large avocado

- ❑ cilantro
- ❑ 1 red bell pepper
- ❑ 1 large lime
- ❑ 1 honeydew melon

- ❑ cornstarch
- ❑ cumin
- ❑ vegetable oil

Lemon Mushroom Sole
with Fresh Broccoli and French Bread

- ❑ 2 pounds sole fillets
- ❑ grated Parmesan cheese
- ❑ ½ pint heavy cream
- ❑ parsley
- ❑ 12 mushrooms
- ❑ 1 large bunch broccoli
- ❑ 1 lemon

- ❑ French bread

- ❑ butter or margarine
- ❑ dry bread crumbs
- ❑ flour
- ❑ sherry

Week 3 Ingredients Lists

Dollie's Chicken with Stir Fried Vegetables and Parmesan Baked Potato Slices

- ❑ 8 boneless, skinned chicken breasts
- ❑ grated Parmesan cheese
- ❑ 1 head garlic
- ❑ 1 large onion
- ❑ 10 cherry tomatoes
- ❑ 4 baking potatoes

- ❑ 1 cup bean sprouts
- ❑ 3 medium carrots
- ❑ 1 zucchini

- ❑ butter or margarine
- ❑ vegetable oil

Italian Spaghetti with Green Salad and Focaccia

- ❑ 1 pound lean ground beef
- ❑ 2 9-ounce packages fresh spaghetti
- ❑ grated Parmesan cheese
- ❑ 26-ounce jar spaghetti sauce
- ❑ 1 bunch green onions

- ❑ lettuce or romaine
- ❑ focaccia bread

- ❑ olive oil
- ❑ salad dressing
- ❑ vegetable oil

Week 3 Groceries

- [ ] 1   pound lean ground beef
- [ ] 1¼   pound sirloin steak
- [ ] 10–12   boneless, skinned chicken thighs
- [ ] 2   pounds sole fillets
- [ ] 8   boneless, skinned chicken breasts

- [ ] 10   8-inch flour tortillas
- [ ] 2   9-ounce packages fresh spaghetti

- [ ] 5   ounces grated Parmesan cheese
- [ ] 1   26-ounce jar spaghetti sauce
- [ ] 1   small can green chiles
- [ ] ½   pint light sour cream
- [ ] ½   pint heavy cream
- [ ] 3   14½-ounce cans chicken broth
- [ ] 1   3-ounce package slivered almonds

- [ ] 1   head garlic
- [ ] 2   large onions
- [ ] 1   large bunch green onions
- [ ] 1   head lettuce or romaine
- [ ] 3   medium Roma tomatoes
- [ ] 1   large avocado
- [ ] 1   bunch parsley
- [ ] 1   bunch cilantro
- [ ] 12   mushrooms
- [ ] 10   cherry tomatoes
- [ ] 4   baking potatoes
- [ ] 1   cup bean sprouts
- [ ] 1   pound snow peas
- [ ] 1   red bell pepper
- [ ] 6   medium carrots
- [ ] 1   small bunch celery
- [ ] 1   large bunch broccoli
- [ ] 1   zucchini
- [ ] 1   large lime

- ☐ 1   honeydew melon
- ☐ 1   lemon

- ☐ 1   loaf French bread
- ☐ 1   loaf focaccia bread

Check:

- ☐ brown sugar
- ☐ butter/margarine
- ☐ cornstarch
- ☐ cumin
- ☐ dry bread crumbs
- ☐ flour
- ☐ olive oil
- ☐ raw rice
- ☐ salad dressing
- ☐ salt and fresh ground black pepper
- ☐ sesame oil
- ☐ sherry
- ☐ soy sauce
- ☐ toasted sesame seeds
- ☐ vegetable oil

Week 4

Pasta Carbonara ?
with Green Salad and Fresh Orange Slices

🍐

Titanic Turkey Stir Fry ?
with Apple Slices

🍐

Baked Flank Steak ?
with Bulgar Wheat Pilaf, Fresh Carrots,
? and Green Salad

🍐

Angel Hair Pasta with Crab ?
Green Salad, and French Bread

🍐

Yakitori Chicken ?
with Chinese Breakfast Noodles

Oh, Canada!

John and I count among our favorite friends a unique Canadian, who is equal parts athlete, humorist, businessman, and practical joker. When we first met our friend John, this ex-rugby player was proprietor of a hotel in bustling downtown Victoria, British Columbia, and spent his weekends at home on Salt Spring Island in the Canadian San Juans, where sheep grazed and chickens squawked in the henhouse. Tennis had long ago replaced rugby as his sporting passion, and John had built three tennis courts right in the middle of this pastoral setting—one a hard surface, one grass, and the third an indoor court. This hospitable man frequently invited us, along with some of our tennis-playing friends, for hotly contested Canadian-American challenge matches on the three courts. John loved watching us scramble after his tricky array of drop shots, spins, and slices on the various surfaces. No one was a stranger to J.O., who often greeted new arrivals with, "Hi, I'm John. How do you like me so far?"

Two artificial hips later, golf has replaced tennis as his favorite athletic pursuit, and John and his wife, Carmen, now spend their winters in the warmth of the California desert among palm trees, manicured grass, and immaculate gardens. But John never forgets his roots, and his bright red, customized golf cart proudly flies two little flags—one Canadian and one U.S. Ever the athlete, John would love to "carbo load" on this entree.

Pasta Carbonara
with Green Salad and Fresh Orange Slices

SERVES 4

Percentage of total
calories from the
following categories:

Protein: 19%
Carbohydrate: 47%
Fat: 34%

INGREDIENTS

½ pound lean bacon
½ cup chopped parsley
2 9-ounce packages fresh linguini
2 eggs

2 tablespoons olive oil
1 tablespoon bacon drippings
½ cup grated Parmesan cheese

GREEN SALAD

1 head lettuce or romaine
2 ~~3 4~~ green onions

salad dressing

FRUIT SIDE DISH

3 large oranges

1. For pasta, fill a large pot with water and begin to heat.
2. Prepare ingredients:
   • Slice and chop bacon into small squares.
   • Chop parsley.
3. For fruit, cut both ends off of an orange with a sharp knife. Stand orange upright on a cutting board and, starting at the top, slice down and around the sides just under the skin, until all skin is removed. Turn orange on its side and cut in ¼- to ½-inch slices, then place on a serving dish. Repeat. Slices will look like pinwheels.
4. For green salad, wash and dry lettuce, then chop and place in a bowl. Slice green onions, including tops, and add to salad bowl.
5. For pasta, fry the bacon squares until crisp, stirring occasionally so that the pieces cook evenly. Drain on paper towels, reserving 1 tablespoon of the drippings.
6. Cook pasta in boiling, salted water 3 to 4 minutes or until done.
7. While pasta is still warm, return to pot and turn burner to low. Add beaten eggs and toss lightly and quickly.
8. Remove pot from heat and add olive oil and bacon drippings, then toss lightly again.
9. Add parsley, bacon, and Parmesan cheese, and toss again. Pasta Carbonara can be served at room temperature.
10. To complete green salad, add dressing to greens and toss lightly. Serve on individual plates.

Hint

To save time when you're making green salad, only buy romaine hearts. Wash them as soon as you get home from the grocery store, and keep them wrapped in paper towels in your refrigerator.

WEEK 4

K.T.

With her baseball cap playfully backwards, Katie Huguenin is one of daughter Julie's closest friends. Katie's mom is an old college friend of mine, and we got our little girls together for the first of many father-daughter tennis matches when they were just six years old. A love of the sport grew along with the friendship, and ironically both girls ended up playing on their college tennis teams. The dads now scramble for points on the court.

Although they attended high schools in different cities and colleges in different states, Julie and Katie share a fun-loving, unspoiled view of the world, and they call each other frequently to discuss important stuff like *guys*. In a recent development for one of them, a young man named Christian has moved securely into the top spot, while the appeal of a certain local basketball player still endures for the other. But stay tuned ...

Katie is always a welcome guest at our house and was recently over for dinner and an overnight. Around 9:00 P.M. the girls decided a late movie would be fun, and they invited John and me along. Flattered to be included, but not wanting to admit that the late show meant getting home long past our normal bedtime, we joined them. For obvious reasons Katie later suggested renaming the evening's entree.

Titanic Turkey Stir Fry
with Apple Slices

SERVES 4

Percentage of total
calories from the
following categories:

Protein: 26%
Carbohydrate: 50%
Fat: 24%

INGREDIENTS

1 large piece of turkey breast
1 bunch broccoli
3 large carrots
½ 1 onion
¾ teaspoon chicken bouillon

2 cloves garlic
3 tablespoons oil
1 16-ounce package Marco Polo Chinese noodles
½ cup sliced almonds

MARINADE

1 tablespoon soy sauce
1 tablespoon sherry

2 teaspoons cornstarch

FRUIT SIDE DISH

3 green apples

1. For turkey entree, mix soy sauce, sherry, and cornstarch in a bowl.
2. Cut turkey into small pieces and place in marinade. Stir until all turkey pieces are coated.
3. Prepare ingredients:
   - Trim stalks off broccoli and cut into small flowerets.
   - Peel carrots and slice thinly on the diagonal.
   - Peel and quarter onion, then slice very thinly.
4. Fill a large pot with water and begin to heat for Chinese noodles.
5. For fruit, slice green apples and place on a serving plate.
6. For turkey entree, heat 1 tablespoon oil in a wide frying pan or wok over medium-high heat. Stir fry onion for 2 minutes, then add carrot slices and broccoli. Stir fry 2 more minutes.
7. Mix chicken bouillon with ¾ cup boiling water and add to vegetables; cook another 2 to 3 minutes until all vegetables are tender-crisp. Remove from pan and set aside.
8. Place Chinese noodles in boiling water.
9. Add 2 tablespoons oil to wok. Press garlic and add marinated turkey pieces. Stir fry until turkey is cooked through.
10. Add vegetable mixture and toss together. Add almonds at the last minute.
11. Remove Chinese noodles from heat, drain in a colander, and rinse. Place individual servings of noodles on plates, then spoon turkey and vegetables on top and serve immediately.

Hint

Here's a good family rule: If your non-cooking spouse or children ask about dinnertime or want to sample the food, they must then assume some responsibility for the meal by making the salad, setting the table, or stirring the pasta. As the cook, you'll either be left alone OR you'll get the help you need!

WEEK 4

Oops!

Everyone makes mistakes. I was out for the day and called home to ask teenage daughter Jill to take a pork roast out of the freezer. The preparation instructions I gave her were very specific and she followed them dutifully, except for one major oversight. Despite differences in the size, shape, and color of the two cuts of meat, she managed to confuse a flank steak with a pork roast. But everyone liked the result so much that I added it to the menu system.

Baked Flank Steak

with Bulgar Wheat Pilaf, Fresh Carrots, and Green Salad

SERVES 4

Percentage of total
calories from the
following categories:

Protein: 26%
Carbohydrate: 37%
Fat: 37%

INGREDIENTS

1½ pound flank steak

salt, garlic salt, and
ground pepper

BULGAR PILAF

3 stalks celery

½ 1 onion

3 tablespoons butter or margarine

2 cups bulgar wheat

4 cups chicken broth

VEGETABLE SIDE DISH

4–5 carrots

butter or margarine

GREEN SALAD

1 head lettuce or romaine

2 3–4 green onions

salad dressing

1. Preheat oven to 350 degrees.
2. For flank steak, place steak in a 9 x 13-inch roasting pan and sprinkle liberally with salt, garlic salt, and freshly ground black pepper.
3. For pilaf, prepare vegetables:
   • Peel and quarter onion, then slice very thinly.
   • Finely chop celery stalks.
4. Melt butter in a large frying pan over medium-high heat. Add celery, onion, and bulgar and stir until bulgar is golden brown.
5. For flank steak, place meat in oven and bake 20 minutes until still pink in the center.
6. For pilaf, add chicken broth to bulgar and vegetables. When broth begins a rolling boil, lower heat and cover. Simmer for 15 minutes.
7. For green salad, wash and dry lettuce, then chop and place in a salad bowl. Slice green onions, including tops, and add to salad bowl.
8. For vegetable, peel carrots and slice diagonally. Place in a microwave-proof dish and cook on high for 5 minutes. Remove and add butter or margarine and salt to taste.
9. To complete pilaf, remove from heat and let sit, uncovered. Before serving, fluff with a large spoon.
10. To complete green salad, add dressing to greens and toss lightly. Serve on individual plates.
11. Remove flank steak from oven and slice very thinly on the diagonal. Serve immediately.

Hint

It may sound preposterous, but if you're making a green salad for a big group, place the washed greens in a zippered pillowcase cover or net mesh bag. Then put the bag in the washing machine on spin dry cycle. Voila! Thoroughly dry greens ready to be dressed!

WEEK 4

One-two-three, One-two-three

Seattle hosted the Goodwill Games in the summer of 1990, and many Seattleites had the unique experience of housing a Russian athlete. Our houseguest was Tatiana Nikolevna, a 1968 Olympic gold medalist in women's basketball whose English vocabulary was somewhat sparse, but whose delivery was unusually animated. Tatiana was strong-willed, fiercely opinionated, loyal to her homeland, and she *loved* Kmart.

Tatiana had a very specific shopping agenda, and for two days, she and I scoured the clothing racks at local discount stores searching for bargains for her son, Sergei. Young Sergei, it seems, was a weightlifter of Olympian dimensions: size 55 pants and size 15 shoes. Tatiana had budgeted carefully, but at the end of our shopping excursion she was short of funds to buy him a highly coveted leather jacket. When I told her that I wanted to help her purchase the coveted jacket, she threw her arms around me and gleefully dragged me down the aisle of Sears doing an enthusiastic Russian folk dance. As usual Tatiana was leading—and we must have been quite a sight.

Whenever I prepare this crab dish, I remember Tatiana. She loved our Northwest seafood and particularly enjoyed this pasta dish.

Angel Hair Pasta with Crab
Green Salad and French Bread

Percentage of total calories from the following categories:

Protein: 20%
Carbohydrate: 43%
Fat: 36%

INGREDIENTS

3 medium-sized ripe tomatoes	2 cloves garlic
3 ,6 green onions	2 6-ounce cans lump crab meat
½ cup parsley	or 12 ounces fresh crab
1½ tablespoons fresh lemon juice	2 9-ounce packages fresh angel
2 tablespoons butter or margarine	hair pasta or capellini
2 tablespoons oil	

SALAD

1 head lettuce or romaine   salad dressing
2 3–4 green onions

BREAD

1 loaf French bread

1. Fill a large pot with water and begin to heat for pasta. Preheat oven to 350 degrees.
2. For crab entree, prepare ingredients:
   - Halve tomatoes and squeeze to remove seeds, then chop in small chunks.
   - Chop green onions, including tops, in ¼-inch slices.
   - Chop parsley.
   - Squeeze fresh lemon juice and set aside.
3. For green salad, wash and dry lettuce, then chop for salad and place in a salad bowl. Slice green onions, including tops, and add to salad bowl.
4. Place French bread on a cookie sheet and heat in warm oven.
5. For crab entree, place butter and oil in a wide frying pan or wok over medium-high heat. Press garlic and add to pan along with tomatoes and green onions. Cook, stirring gently, until mixture bubbles, then lower heat and simmer gently for 1 to 2 minutes.
6. Place pasta in boiling water and cook for 1 to 2 minutes.
7. To complete green salad, add dressing to greens and toss lightly. Serve on individual plates.
8. For crab entree, remove pasta from heat and drain in a large colander.
9. Add lemon juice, crab, and parsley to tomato mixture. Cook, stirring just until crab is heated through, for approximately 1 minute.
10. Slice French bread.
11. For crab entree, place individual servings of pasta on plates and spoon tomato-crab mixture on top. Serve immediately.

Hint

Gourmet cooks suggest that an ingredient that adds tremendous interest, taste, and flavor to stir frys, pastas, and salads—and has a good refrigerator shelf life—is green onions.

WEEK 4

Fit to Be Thai'd

Dr. Supat Leelehrismee, a Thai endocrinologist, came to Seattle to study diabetes at Virginia Mason Medical Center for three months. He spent long hours in the lab and medical library and, without his family, endured many lonely evenings in his small apartment. Hoping to broaden his American experience a bit, we invited him over for dinner on two different occasions.

Supat was a tiny man, no more than 5'4" with a very slight build. The first night he came to our house I served him a typical American meal. Supat ate modestly, answered our questions in careful English, and declined dessert. A month later he came back for a second visit, and I decided to serve an Asian entree accompanied by Chinese Breakfast Noodles, a rice noodle side dish flavored with mellow sesame oil and hoisin sauce. Supat's appetite perked right up as he relished the more familiar flavors. He devoured his meal and served himself a full second plate. Then he politely requested that the leftovers be packed up so that he could take them home.

Supat liked the entree because of its Asian accent. I like it because the preparation is so easy. The original recipe was for chicken kabobs, but one evening I didn't have enough time to thread all the skewers, so I simply tossed the ingredients together in a wok. The result isn't nearly as aesthetic, but it has Dr. Supat's endorsement.

Yakitori Chicken
with Chinese Breakfast Noodles

SERVES 4

Percentage of total calories from the following categories:

Protein: 19%
Carbohydrate: 50%
Fat: 31%

INGREDIENTS

4 boneless, skinned chicken
     breasts
1 large green pepper

10 mushrooms
1 pineapple

MARINADE

3 tablespoons oil
¼ cup brown sugar

⅓ cup bottled teriyaki sauce

SIDE DISH OF CHINESE NOODLES

16 ounces Chinese egg noodles
1 tablespoon oyster sauce
3 tablespoons light soy sauce

1 tablespoon toasted sesame seeds
2 tablespoons sesame oil
2 green onions

1. For chicken marinade, combine oil, brown sugar, and teriyaki sauce in a medium bowl.
2. Cut chicken breasts into thin slices, then into 1-inch pieces. Place in marinade.
3. Prepare vegetables:
   • Trim green pepper and cut into chunks.
   • Trim stems and quarter mushrooms.
4. For Chinese noodles, fill a large pot with water and heat.
5. For chicken entree, slice ends off pineapple, then cut pineapple in half lengthwise. Cut both halves in half to make four quarters. Trim center rind off of each quarter and cut quarters in half. Remove rind from each piece, leaving a thick spear of pineapple. Cut each spear into ½-inch pieces.
6. For Chinese noodles, mix oyster sauce, light soy, and sesame oil in a small bowl. Chop green onions.
7. For chicken entree, pour chicken and marinade into a wide frying pan or wok, reserving 1 tablespoon of the marinade. Cook for 4 to 5 minutes over medium-high heat until chicken is almost done. Remove chicken and set aside.
8. For Chinese noodles, place noodles in boiling water and cook for approximately 4 minutes until done.

Continued next page . . .

Hint

Did you know pasta can be cooked ahead? Just run hot/boiling water over it in a strainer to get it ready to serve at a later time.

WEEK 4

Note: If possible, marinate the chicken in the morning.

Yakitori Chicken

CONTINUED . . .

9. For chicken entree, add remaining 1 tablespoon of marinade to frying pan and cook mushrooms for 1 minute. Add green pepper and pineapple. Toss until heated through, approximately 1 to 2 minutes. Drain well.

10. For Chinese noodles, remove noodles from heat and drain in a large colander. Toss gently with sauce. Place individual servings on plates and sprinkle with sesame seeds and chopped green onion.

11. Drain chicken and place back in wok with vegetables and pineapple. Toss briefly. Serve immediately using a slotted spoon.

WEEK 4

Advice

FOR LITTLE ONES

- With toddlers, stick to one-word reminders: "Shoes," "Lights" (off), "Water bottle," etc. This avoids the agitation of more long-winded reminders and is even more effective than going on and on at length.

- Make Saturday "Candy Day" when your children are small. They can each pick one pack of gum or one candy and that's it for the week. They'll never ask for more, and will always look forward to Saturdays. If they receive candy during the week, they must save it for Saturday.

- Here are two easy at-home birthday party ideas. For a Pajama Pancake Party, cover the table with butcher paper and let kids draw their own place mats within large squares or rectangles that you have previously traced at their seats. Mom and Dad have to be in their PJs, too. For a Tea Party, Mom and Dad dress as a maid and butler. Serve tea sandwiches, fruits, and mints, and play old-fashioned games such as remembering tea/kitchen items on a tray, unscrambling scrambled "tea" words, or guessing the number of clothespins in a jar.

- To make grocery shopping easier, cut out grocery store coupons and play a "hide and seek" game for your children. Organize the coupons by store aisles, and when you go shopping, give your kids the coupons for a particular aisle and they have to "find" the products. You, meanwhile, will shop in peace and quiet.

Week 4 Ingredients Lists

Pasta Carbonara with Green Salad and Fresh Orange Slices

- ½ pound lean bacon
- 2 9-ounce packages fresh linguini
- 5 ounces grated Parmesan cheese
- lettuce or romaine
- 1 bunch green onions
- parsley
- 3 large oranges
- eggs
- olive oil
- salad dressing

Titanic Turkey Stir Fry with Apple Slices

- 1 pound turkey breast
- 16-ounce package Marco Polo noodles
- 3-ounce package sliced almonds
- 1 head garlic
- 1 large onion
- 1 large bunch broccoli
- 3 large carrots
- 3 green apples
- chicken bouillon
- cornstarch
- sherry
- soy sauce
- vegetable oil

Baked Flank Steak with Bulgar Wheat Pilaf, Fresh Carrots, and Green Salad

- 1½-pound flank steak
- 1 package bulgar wheat
- 3 14½-ounce cans chicken broth
- lettuce or romaine
- 1 bunch green onions
- 1 onion
- 1 small bunch celery
- 5 carrots
- butter or margarine
- garlic salt
- salad dressing

Week 4 Ingredients Lists

Angel Hair Pasta with Crab, Green Salad, and French Bread

- ❏ 2 9-ounce packages angel hair pasta
- ❏ 2 6-ounce cans lump crab meat (no leg meat)
- ❏ 1 head garlic
- ❏ lettuce or romaine
- ❏ 1 bunch green onions
- ❏ 3 medium ripe tomatoes

- ❏ parsley
- ❏ 1 lemon
- ❏ French bread

- ❏ butter or margarine
- ❏ salad dressing
- ❏ vegetable oil

Yakitori Chicken with Chinese Breakfast Noodles

- ❏ 4 boneless, skinned chicken breasts
- ❏ 16-ounce package Chinese egg noodles
- ❏ 1 bunch green onions
- ❏ 1 green pepper
- ❏ 10 mushrooms
- ❏ 1 pineapple

- ❏ brown sugar
- ❏ light soy sauce
- ❏ oyster sauce
- ❏ sesame oil
- ❏ teriyaki sauce
- ❏ toasted sesame seeds
- ❏ vegetable oil

Week 4 Groceries

- [ ] ½ pound lean bacon
- [ ] 1 large fresh turkey breast (approximately 1 pound)
- [ ] 1½ pound flank steak
- [ ] 4 boneless, skinned chicken breasts

- [ ] 1 16-ounce package Marco Polo Chinese noodles
- [ ] 1 16-ounce package Chinese egg noodles
- [ ] 2 9-ounce packages fresh linguini
- [ ] 2 9-ounce packages angel hair pasta

- [ ] 5 ounces grated Parmesan cheese
- [ ] 2 6-ounce cans lump crab meat (no leg meat)
- [ ] 1 3-ounce package sliced almonds
- [ ] 1 package bulgar wheat
- [ ] 3 14½-ounce cans chicken broth

- [ ] 1 head garlic
- [ ] 3 heads lettuce or romaine
- [ ] 3 bunches green onions
- [ ] 3 medium ripe tomatoes
- [ ] 2 onions
- [ ] 1 bunch parsley
- [ ] 1 small bunch celery
- [ ] 1 green pepper
- [ ] 10 mushrooms
- [ ] 1 large bunch broccoli
- [ ] 8 large carrots
- [ ] 3 large oranges
- [ ] 1 lemon
- [ ] 1 pineapple
- [ ] 3 green apples

- [ ] 1 loaf French bread

Check:

- [ ] brown sugar
- [ ] butter/margarine
- [ ] chicken bouillon
- [ ] cornstarch
- [ ] eggs
- [ ] garlic salt
- [ ] light soy sauce
- [ ] oyster sauce
- [ ] salad dressing
- [ ] salt and fresh ground black pepper
- [ ] sesame oil
- [ ] sherry
- [ ] soy sauce
- [ ] teriyaki sauce
- [ ] toasted sesame seeds
- [ ] vegetable oil

Week 5

Chicken Stroganoff with Linguini ✳
and Green Salad

Flank Steak with Bok Choy ?
and Fresh Pineapple

Turkey Spaghetti Marinara ✳
with Green Salad and Bread Sticks

Shrimp Pesto Stir Fry with Rice ?
and Watermelon Slices

Liz's Honey-Baked Chicken ✳
with Healthy Mashed Potatoes and Spinach

Camping with the Ladies

I couldn't say no to attending a four-day golf camp with three close women friends at Black Butte Ranch, a working cattle ranch high in the Cascade Mountains of beautiful central Oregon. The ranch sits in a pastoral meadow surrounded by jagged mountains. Heathery spring colors were in full bloom for our May visit, and we had a wonderful time.

The four of us drove down to Oregon together, my Volkswagen van crammed with all the necessities: golf clubs, tennis racquets, bicycles, running shoes, playing cards, and (because we're from Seattle) an espresso machine. Our days were filled with exercise; our evenings with relaxed card games, and conversation. The cooking responsibilities were shared, and we ate extremely well. Two of my camp-mates were in the food business—one was a restaurant owner and the second operated a thriving cookie and candy-making business. When it was my turn to cook, I prepared a recipe I devised a few years ago. I had always loved rich beef stroganoff and had experimented with a lighter, healthier version made with chicken and a colorful medley of vegetables. I have modified Chicken Stroganoff over the years, cutting down on the butter and using light sour cream instead of regular; this reduces the calories and fat content but doesn't impact the flavor.

I'm flattered when these friends requested a recipe, and I was glad to share this one.

Chicken Stroganoff with Linguini
and Green Salad

SERVES 4

Percentage of total
calories from the
following categories:

Protein: 21%
Carbohydrate: 43%
Fat: 36%

INGREDIENTS

4 boneless, skinned chicken breasts
2 1 bunch green onions
1 dozen mushrooms
10 cherry tomatoes
3 tablespoons butter or margarine

4 cloves garlic
2 9-ounce packages fresh
   linguini
½ cup light sour cream
salt and pepper to taste

GREEN SALAD

1 head lettuce or romaine
1 navel orange

salad dressing

1. For stroganoff, prepare ingredients:
   - Cut chicken breasts into thin strips, then into 1-inch pieces.
   - Thinly slice green onions, including tops.
   - Trim stems from mushrooms and slice thinly.
   - Halve cherry tomatoes.
2. Fill a large pot with water and begin to heat for pasta.
3. For green salad, wash and dry lettuce, then chop and place in a salad bowl. Add a few of the green onions that were sliced for the stroganoff. Peel the orange and cut sections into bite-sized pieces, then add to salad bowl.
4. For stroganoff, melt butter in a wide frying pan or wok over medium-high heat. Press garlic into pan and saute briefly. Add cut-up chicken pieces, green onion, and mushrooms, and cook until chicken is done, stirring frequently. Remove from heat.
5. Place fresh linguini in boiling water and cook 1 to 2 minutes or until done.
6. To complete green salad, add dressing to greens and toss lightly. Serve on individual plates.
7. For stroganoff, put chicken and vegetable mixture back on burner and add sour cream, and salt and pepper to taste. Add cherry tomato halves and toss gently until heated through.
8. Remove pasta from heat and drain in a large colander. Place individual servings of pasta on plates. Spoon stroganoff sauce on top and serve immediately.

Hint

Capers add a lot of zip to salad dressings. To easily remove them from their skinny jars, tilt the jar slightly and use a vegetable peeler to remove the capers, a few at a time. They will line up in the peeler without rolling out, and the liquid drains back into the jar.

WEEK 5

Why Does <u>She</u> Have All the Luck?

A number of years ago, our good friends Fred and Nina Fogg went on a business trip and left high school-age daughters Cara and Randi with us for a few days. Beautiful, spirited Cara has now graduated from Boston College, where stories of her silver-lining misadventures abound. First, there was the time she and some friends traveled to South Bend for the BC vs. Notre Dame football game. Arriving without tickets for the sold-out game, they somehow ended up with seats on the 40-yard line and a visit to the Irish locker room after the game.

Then there was her spring break trip to Europe as a college senior. Cara and another friend missed the train out of Florence that was to take them to Geneva for the flight home to Boston. The Boston airport, however, was snowed in, and the flight she missed had actually been cancelled. That meant two extra days on the Italian Riviera, with no penalty for missing the original flight. Some people have all the luck.

When Cara stayed with us, I knew she wasn't very fond of fresh vegetables, but I served her bok choy anyway. This mild, leafy green with the crisp, watery stalk was a hit. Her enthusiasm might just have been her good manners talking, but she was convincing.

Flank Steak with Bok Choy
and Fresh Pineapple

SERVES 4

Percentage of total
calories from the
following categories:

Protein: 26%
Carbohydrate: 44%
Fat: 30%

INGREDIENTS

1¼ pound flank steak	2 cloves garlic
1 head bok choy	½ cup water
3 tablespoons oil	1 16-ounce package Marco Polo Chinese noodles

MARINADE

¼ cup soy sauce	2 teaspoons sugar
1 tablespoon sherry	2 tablespoons cornstarch

FRUIT SIDE DISH

1 large pineapple

1. For flank steak entree, combine soy sauce, sherry, sugar, and cornstarch in a medium bowl.
2. Slice flank steak thinly across the grain, then cut slices in 1-inch pieces. Place meat slices in marinade and stir to coat meat.
3. Trim stem end off of bok choy, then slice stalks and leafy tops thinly.
4. Fill a large pot with water and begin to heat for Chinese noodles.
5. For fruit, slice both ends off of pineapple and cut in half lengthwise, then cut both halves in half to make quarters. Trim center rind off of each quarter, then cut quarters in half. Remove rind from each piece, leaving a thick spear of pineapple. Cut each spear in ½-inch chunks and place in a serving bowl.
6. For flank steak entree, heat 1 tablespoon oil in a wide frying pan or wok over medium-high heat and press garlic into pan. Add bok choy and stir fry for 2 minutes. Add water and stir fry 1 minute more. Remove from pan and set aside.
7. Add Chinese noodles to boiling water and cook 5 minutes or until done.
8. Heat 2 tablespoons oil in the frying pan and stir fry beef 3 minutes or until barely pink.
9. Add bok choy and broth, and simmer until a sauce forms.
10. Remove Chinese noodles and drain in a large colander. Place individual servings on plates and spoon beef and bok choy on top. Serve immediately.

Hint

When marinating beef or chicken, do so in a zip-lock bag. Place the plastic bag in a bowl for support and then measure marinade ingredients directly into the bag. The meat or chicken will be easy to turn and you won't have an extra pan or bowl to wash.

WEEK 5

Double Trouble

Daughter Jill fell in love her sophomore year in college with Justin Piasecki, the guy next door. The dorm room next door, that is. There was no stopping this freight train of a romance, and now we couldn't ask for a more wonderful son-in-law.

Justin was raised in picturesque, rural Vermont and has an identical twin brother named Dana. When they chose colleges, the previously inseparable pair parted, with Dana on the East Coast and Justin in California. A week before Jill and Justin's senior-year wedding, the whole Piasecki family arrived in Seattle for the first time, and came over for an informal dinner.

Justin and Dana have since taken two years off from graduate school to train for the 2000 Olympics in doubles flatwater sprint kayaking, but I knew they were serious athletes following a serious training regimen even in those college days. What I didn't quite comprehend was the amount of food the twins could consume. I had prepared what I thought would be an ample quantity of Turkey Spaghetti Marinara and the pasta was steaming in the pot when I summoned everyone for dinner. "Justin and Dana," I said politely, "why don't you two go first." Mom Linda, the no-nonsense New Englander, looked at me with a sympathetic shake of her head and cautioned, "That might not be a very good idea."

Fortunately I had two extra packages of fresh pasta in the freezer. I could have used more.

Turkey Spaghetti Marinara
with Green Salad and Bread Sticks

SERVES 4

Percentage of total
calories from the
following categories:

Protein: 21%
Carbohydrate: 55%
Fat: 24%

INGREDIENTS

½ 1 onion
1 carrot
3 mushrooms
2 tablespoons chopped parsley
1 tablespoon olive oil
2 cloves garlic
1 teaspoon basil
½ teaspoon rosemary, oregano,
    and salt

1 pound ground turkey
1 28-ounce can Italian-style
    tomatoes
1 6-ounce can tomato paste
¼ cup white wine
1 bay leaf
1 teaspoon sugar
2 9-ounce packages fresh spaghetti
    grated Parmesan cheese

GREEN SALAD

1 head lettuce or romaine
2 3-4 green onions

salad dressing

BREAD

8–12 bread sticks

1. For turkey entree, prepare vegetables:
   • Peel and quarter onion, then slice very thinly.
   • Peel carrot and grate coarsely.
   • Remove stems from mushrooms and slice thinly.
   • Finely chop parsley.
2. For green salad, wash and dry lettuce, then chop and place in a salad bowl. Slice green onions, including tops, and add to salad bowl.
3. For turkey entree, heat olive oil in a wide frying pan over medium-high heat. Press garlic and add, along with onion, carrot, mushrooms, parsley, basil, rosemary, oregano, and salt. Cook, stirring often, about 4 to 5 minutes or until onion is soft.
4. Crumble ground turkey into the pan and cook, stirring frequently, until turkey is no longer pink.
5. Slice Italian tomatoes thickly and add to pan, along with the tomato liquid, tomato paste, wine, bay leaf, and sugar. Bring sauce to a gentle boil, then lower heat and simmer for 20 minutes, stirring occasionally.

Continued next page . . .

Hint

Many homemade salad dressings are great over blanched fresh vegetables or pasta served at room temperature.

WEEK 5

Turkey Spaghetti Marinara

6. Meanwhile, fill a large pot with water and begin to heat for pasta.
7. When sauce is done, add fresh spaghetti to boiling water and cook approximately 2 to 3 minutes until done.
8. To complete green salad, add dressing and toss lightly. Serve on individual plates.
9. For turkey entree, remove pasta from heat and drain in a large colander. Serve marinara over individual servings of spaghetti and sprinkle with grated Parmesan cheese.

FOR MIDDLE ONES

- To encourage young children to save money, agree to automatically match whatever they save and then place the entire amount in the stock market or a money market fund where children can watch it grow. Nothing encourages saving like observing the magic of compound interest!

- A great place to store your kids' prized schoolwork and artwork is in the clear plastic zippered bags that blankets and pillows come in.

- Involve all the family in household chores by making a chore wheel out of two circles (one larger than the other) of light cardboard, fastened with a grommet in the middle. Put family members' names on the small circle and the chores to be done on the big one. A weekly rotation of the wheel keeps everybody on track.

- For multi-task, whole day seasonal cleaning endeavors, write the jobs on scraps of paper and place them in a jar. Family members then draw out their assignment for the day . . . trading is allowed.

- Use logical consequences. One mom decided her 11-year-old son needed to be responsible for getting up in time to catch the bus for school because, if he missed it, she would have to drive him 12 miles to school. She finally decided to utilize logical consequences and one morning waited until ONE minute before they had to leave for school to waken him. Off he went . . . no shower, no food, no potty. That was the last time he overslept.

A Fear of Needles (and Thread)

We all have our ineptitudes, and sewing heads my list. This lack of skill has made certain times of year (like Halloween) a little humiliating, as my kids canvassed neighborhood candy bowls on that much-anticipated evening wearing their usual "hobo" attire.

But it wasn't just Halloween. When daughter Julie came home from middle-school tryouts for the musical *The Wizard of Oz* and announced that she had been chosen to play the Tin Man, I was immediately concerned about the costume. Fortunately, after a lengthy search, I located a Tin Man costume on sale for half-price at a local costume store. At that point, I would have paid double for it.

I may not be creative with a needle and thread, but open up your refrigerator door and I can probably create something out of the odds and ends inside. That's how Shrimp Pesto Stir Fry came to be. In addition to the frozen shrimp I came across in the freezer one day, I found a sampling of fresh vegetables in the cooler section and a container of prepared pesto. This was the colorful result.

Shrimp Pesto Stir Fry with Rice
and Watermelon Slices

SERVES 4

Percentage of total calories from the following categories:

Protein: 21%
Carbohydrate: 55%
Fat: 24%

INGREDIENTS

2½ cups raw rice
1 onion
1 small zucchini
8–10 mushrooms
½ red bell pepper
1 carrot

2 tablespoons butter or
    margarine
3 tablespoons prepared
    pesto sauce
¾ pound baby shrimp

FRUIT SIDE DISH

¼ watermelon

Hint

Small amounts (tablespoons) of pesto or tomato paste can be frozen in sandwich baggies or ice cube trays.

1. For shrimp entree, rinse rice and prepare according to package directions.
2. Prepare vegetables:
   - Peel, quarter, and slice onion thinly.
   - Trim ends off of zucchini, quarter lengthwise, and slice thinly.
   - Trim stems off of mushrooms and slice thinly.
   - Cut red pepper in thin strips.
   - Peel carrot and cut in thin, diagonal slices.
3. For fruit, cut watermelon in 1-inch slices and place on a serving dish.
4. For shrimp entree, place 1 tablespoon butter in a wide frying pan or wok over medium-high heat. Add onion and carrot, and stir fry for 2 minutes. Add zucchini, mushrooms, and red pepper. Cook approximately 2 more minutes, just until vegetables are tender-crisp.
5. Add remaining 1 tablespoon butter to pan; stir in pesto sauce.
6. Add shrimp and heat through, approximately 30 seconds.
7. Return vegetables to pan and stir until vegetables are coated with pesto. Serve immediately over rice.

"Oh, Say, Can You See"

Every parent experiences moments of magic—brief interactions with our children that we don't want to end.

A number of years ago, we had the pleasure of hosting two young French sisters for three days. Their father coached a women's basketball team from France that was playing in a tournament here. Florence and Violaine came along for the trip, staying with us for a few days and attending school with Jill and Julie.

The foursome, all in their early teens, hit it off spectacularly, talking and giggling until late each night. The evening before the sisters returned to France, they all stayed up particularly late. It was nearing midnight on a school night when I peered into Jill's bedroom. The four girls were sitting cross-legged on Jill's bed. One would speak slowly and distinctly in her native language, enunciating carefully, and the others would repeat the words. Then they all would laugh and sing loudly. I stood quietly in the doorway as these happy young teenagers, two Americans and two French, taught each other their national anthems. It was a magic moment.

We enjoyed a number of dinners with our French guests, but this was Florence and Violaine's favorite.

Liz's Honey-Baked Chicken
with Healthy Mashed Potatoes and Spinach

SERVES 4

Percentage of total
calories from the
following categories:

Protein: 31%
Carbohydrate: 35%
Fat: 33%

INGREDIENTS

½ cup butter or margarine
½ cup honey
¼ cup prepared mustard

1 teaspoon curry powder
8 boneless, skinned chicken breasts
salt and pepper

MASHED POTATO SIDE DISH

4 baking potatoes
salt and pepper

milk

VEGETABLE SIDE DISH

1 10-ounce package frozen spinach

1. Preheat oven to 350 degrees.
2. For chicken entree, melt butter in a small bowl in the microwave, then add honey, mustard, and curry.
3. Place chicken breasts on a rimmed cookie sheet. Spoon honey-mustard sauce on top. Place chicken in preheated oven and bake about 25 minutes or until done.
4. For mashed potatoes, heat 2 inches of salted water to boiling in a large saucepan or Dutch oven. Wash potatoes and cut in chunks, leaving skins on. Place potato chunks in water and cook approximately 15 to 20 minutes until done.
5. For vegetable, place frozen spinach in a microwave-proof dish and cook on high for 8 minutes.
6. For mashed potatoes, drain potatoes and beat with a hand mixer, adding milk until the desired consistency. Salt and pepper to taste.
7. For vegetable, remove spinach from microwave and drain thoroughly. Butter lightly, then add salt and pepper to taste.

Hint

If you prefer baked potatoes to mashed, but turn up your nose at soggy microwaved potatoes, try a combination method. Microwave the scrubbed potatoes on high for 4 minutes, then bake them in a pre-heated 450 degree oven for 20 minutes. The result will be a fluffy potato with dry, crispy skin in less than half the time.

WEEK 5

Week 5 Ingredients Lists

Chicken Stroganoff with Linguini and Green Salad

- [ ] 4 boneless, skinned chicken breasts
- [ ] 2 9-ounce packages fresh linguine
- [ ] ½ pint sour cream
- [ ] 1 head garlic
- [ ] lettuce or romaine
- [ ] 1 bunch green onions
- [ ] 10 cherry tomatoes
- [ ] 1 dozen mushrooms
- [ ] 1 orange
- [ ] butter or margarine
- [ ] salad dressing

Flank Steak with Bok Choy and Fresh Pineapple

- [ ] 1¼-pound flank steak
- [ ] 16-ounce package Marco Polo Chinese noodles
- [ ] 1 head garlic
- [ ] 1 large head bok choy
- [ ] 1 pineapple
- [ ] cornstarch
- [ ] sherry
- [ ] soy sauce
- [ ] sugar
- [ ] vegetable oil

Turkey Spaghetti Marinara with Green Salad and Bread Sticks

- [ ] 1 pound fresh ground turkey
- [ ] 29-ounce package fresh spaghetti
- [ ] 5 ounces grated Parmesan cheese
- [ ] 28-ounce can Italian-style tomatoes
- [ ] 6-ounce can tomato paste
- [ ] 1 head garlic
- [ ] lettuce or romaine
- [ ] 1 bunch green onions
- [ ] 1 onion
- [ ] parsley
- [ ] 1 carrot
- [ ] 3 mushrooms
- [ ] bread sticks
- [ ] basil
- [ ] bay leaf
- [ ] olive oil
- [ ] oregano
- [ ] rosemary
- [ ] salad dressing
- [ ] white wine

Week 5 Ingredients Lists

Shrimp Pesto Stir Fry with Rice and Watermelon Slices

- ❏ ¾ pound baby shrimp
- ❏ small container prepared pesto sauce
- ❏ 1 onion
- ❏ 1 red bell pepper
- ❏ 1 small zucchini
- ❏ 1 carrot

- ❏ 8–10 mushrooms
- ❏ ¼ watermelon

- ❏ butter or margarine
- ❏ raw rice

Liz's Honey-Baked Chicken with Healthy Mashed Potatoes and Spinach

- ❏ 8 boneless, skinned chicken breasts
- ❏ 10-ounce package frozen spinach
- ❏ 4 baking potatoes

- ❏ butter or margarine
- ❏ curry powder
- ❏ honey
- ❏ milk
- ❏ prepared mustard

Week 5 Groceries

- [ ] ¾   pound baby shrimp
- [ ] 1¼   pound flank steak
- [ ] 1   pound fresh ground turkey
- [ ] 12   boneless, skinned chicken breasts

- [ ] 2   9-ounce packages fresh linguini
- [ ] 2   9-ounce packages fresh spaghetti
- [ ] 1   16-ounce package Marco Polo Chinese noodles

- [ ] 5   ounces grated Parmesan cheese
- [ ] 1   small container prepared pesto sauce
- [ ] 1   28-ounce can Italian-style tomatoes
- [ ] 1   6-ounce can tomato paste

- [ ] ½   pint light sour cream
- [ ] 1   10-ounce package frozen spinach

- [ ] 1   head garlic
- [ ] 2   heads lettuce or romaine
- [ ] 2   bunches green onions
- [ ] 2   onions
- [ ] 10   cherry tomatoes
- [ ] 1   bunch parsley
- [ ] 1   red bell pepper
- [ ] 1   small zucchini
- [ ] 4   baking potatoes
- [ ] 2   carrots
- [ ] 2   dozen mushrooms
- [ ] 1   large head bok choy
- [ ] 1   orange
- [ ] 1   pineapple
- [ ] ¼   watermelon

- [ ] 1   package bread sticks

Check:

- [ ] basil
- [ ] bay leaf
- [ ] butter/margarine
- [ ] cornstarch
- [ ] curry powder
- [ ] honey
- [ ] milk
- [ ] olive oil
- [ ] oregano
- [ ] prepared mustard
- [ ] raw rice
- [ ] rosemary
- [ ] salad dressing
- [ ] salt and fresh ground black pepper
- [ ] sherry
- [ ] soy sauce
- [ ] sugar
- [ ] vegetable oil
- [ ] white wine

Week 6

Parmesan Chicken ✳

with New Potatoes,

Fresh Broccoli, and Green Salad

❧

Indonesian Bami ?

and Fruit Salad

❧

Fisherman's Spaghetti ✳

with Green Salad and French Bread

❧

Beef Tacos

and Fresh Orange Slices ✳

❧

Chicken Cashew with Rice ✦

and Melon Slices

First Date

I'm not sure how the phrase originated, but here in the Northwest people use the term "Tolo" for a girls-ask-boys dance. At Julie's high school, the Tolo is the first dance of the year, and for weeks in advance, the girls anxiously plot who will ask whom, what other couple they will go with, etc. Once the dance is formally announced, the race for a date is on and the planning intensifies. Should we go out to dinner or cook at home? Who has a driver's license, or which lucky mom or dad gets the midnight shift to take everyone home?

For Julie's first Tolo, she and her friends, after considerable deliberation, decided to prepare dinner at the home of one of her friends. The meal had to be foolproof and easy for four nervous teenage girls to prepare.

Parmesan Chicken was a logical solution. Not only does it fit the criteria, it can easily be put together ahead of time and baked at the last minute.

Parmesan Chicken
with New Potatoes, Fresh Broccoli, and Green Salad

INGREDIENTS

6 tablespoons butter or margarine
⅔ cup grated Parmesan cheese
1 teaspoon salt
¼ teaspoon garlic powder

1 cup dry bread crumbs
8 boneless, skinned chicken
   breasts
1 lemon

POTATO SIDE DISH

6–8 red-skinned potatoes
    butter or margarine
       to taste

light sour cream
salt and fresh cracked black
   pepper

VEGETABLE SIDE DISH

1 large bunch broccoli

butter or margarine to taste

GREEN SALAD

1 head lettuce or romaine
2 3-4 green onions

salad dressing

1. Preheat oven to 350 degrees.
2. For potatoes, heat 2 inches of water to boiling in a large saucepan or Dutch oven. Scrub new potatoes and add to saucepan. Cover, lower heat, and cook for approximately 30 minutes until done.
3. For chicken entree, mix bread crumbs, grated Parmesan cheese, salt, and garlic powder in a pie pan.
4. Melt butter in a glass bowl in the microwave. Dip each breast in butter, and roll in crumb mixture. Place on a rimmed cookie sheet.
5. Squeeze juice of half a lemon over the chicken breasts. Place chicken in oven and bake 20 to 25 minutes or until done.
6. For vegetable, wash, trim, and cut broccoli into spears. Place in a microwave-proof dish.
7. For green salad, wash and dry lettuce, then chop and place in a salad bowl. Slice green onions, including tops, and add to salad bowl.
8. For vegetable, cook broccoli in the microwave for approximately 8 minutes or until tender-crisp. Season with a small amount of butter, and salt and pepper to taste.
9. To complete green salad, add dressing and toss lightly. Serve on individual plates.
10. To serve potatoes, cut into thick slices, butter lightly, and top with a dollop of light sour cream and freshly ground black pepper.

Hint

Put day-old bread, bread crusts and heels, even crackers in the blender to make crumbs to be used later in recipes. Small amounts can be stored in the freezer.

WEEK 6

It Can't Be Good!

My easygoing husband John rarely complains about anything, but he has quietly made his food preferences known over the years. The ingredients in Indonesian Bami are clearly not on his Top Ten list, so I anticipated an unenthused response the first time I prepared this dish.

"I can't figure out why I like this so much," he grumbled. "It has everything in it I don't like—cabbage, onions, and cooked celery." I'm glad he didn't recognize the leeks.

Indonesian Bami

with Fruit Salad

SERVES 4

Percentage of total
calories from the
following ingredients:

Protein: 22%
Carbohydrate: 53%
Fat: 25%

INGREDIENTS

1 pound flank steak	3 tablespoons oil
2 *3* green onions	2 cloves garlic
1 large leek	¼ teaspoon crushed red
3 stalks celery	pepper
12 ounces dry spaghetti	¼ cup soy sauce

FRUIT SALAD

1 banana	grapes
2 oranges	

1. Fill a large pot with water and begin to heat for pasta.
2. For entree, prepare ingredients:
   - Slice flank steak thinly across the grain, then cut in 1-inch pieces.
   - Trim and slice green onions and leek, including tops.
   - Shred cabbage.
   - Slice celery in thin, diagonal pieces.
3. Break spaghetti in half and cook in boiling water until done. Drain and set aside.
4. For fruit salad, prepare fruits and place in a serving dish.
5. For entree, place 1 tablespoon oil in a wide frying pan or wok over medium-high heat. Press garlic cloves and add, along with red pepper. Add flank steak and stir fry for 2 minutes. Steak should still be pink. Remove meat and juice from pan.
6. Add 1 tablespoon oil to frying pan and add green onions, leeks, cabbage, and celery. Stir fry 2 to 3 minutes or until tender-crisp.
7. Add drained spaghetti, remaining 1 tablespoon oil, and soy sauce, then stir fry 1 minute.
8. Drain juice from meat and return to pan. Toss all together gently and serve immediately.

Hint

Vegetable oil spilled on the floor can be very difficult to clean up. An easy way is to sprinkle a thick layer of flour over the spilled oil. Wait a few minutes for the flour to absorb the oil. Then move the oil around gently with a paper towel and sweep up with a dustpan and broom. Spray the area with window cleaner and wipe away the last traces of oil and flour.

Outfoxing a Fox

John and I had known each other less than a year when we got married and, as a young bride, I was initially daunted by the now-familiar Kirkpatrick family pace. An early hint came when we took a vacation the summer after our wedding to visit some of John's relatives in the Midwest.

Thirty minutes after the wheels of the plane touched down in Milwaukee, we were out on the golf course with Uncle Don, the family jokester and most competitive sportsman. I was quite unprepared for Uncle Don's cunning gamesmanship. "Do you exhale or inhale on your backswing?" he would ask. "Did you notice you're standing a little downhill?" Or, with a sympathetic shake of his head, "I sure wouldn't want *that* lie." Later that afternoon, John discovered the best way to stifle his uncle's teasing banter when he scored his first and only ace. "Holy smoke," Don gasped. "A hole-in-one!" It silenced him for the rest of the round.

A retired college business professor and management consultant, Don has conducted personnel seminars all over the world. He and Aunt Fern have stopped in Seattle during their travels and we always love to see them. The last time they came through, this time on their way to Bangkok, we shared the following meal.

Fisherman's Spaghetti

with Green Salad and French Bread

INGREDIENTS

½ ~~1~~ onion
8 mushrooms
3 Roma tomatoes
2 tablespoons butter or margarine
1 teaspoon oregano
2 6-ounce cans lump crab meat (no leg meat)

¼ pound fresh shrimp
½ cup white wine
2 tablespoons Madeira
1 cup light cream
2 egg yolks
2 9-ounce packages fresh angel hair pasta

GREEN SALAD

1 head lettuce or romaine
3–4 green onions

salad dressing

BREAD

1 loaf French bread

1. For seafood entree, prepare ingredients:
   - Peel and quarter onion, then slice very thinly.
   - Trim stems off of mushrooms, then slice.
   - Cut ends off of tomatoes. Quarter and remove seeds with your thumb, then slice in thin strips.
2. Fill a large pot with water and begin to heat for pasta.
3. Preheat oven to 350 degrees.
4. For green salad, wash and dry lettuce, then chop for salad and place in a salad bowl. Slice green onions, including tops, and add to salad bowl.
5. For seafood entree, melt butter in a wide frying pan or wok over medium-high heat. Add onions and saute 2 to 3 minutes.
6. Add mushrooms and oregano and cook several more minutes, stirring occasionally.
7. Place French bread on a cookie sheet and heat in warm oven.
8. To complete green salad, add dressing and toss lightly. Serve on individual plates.
9. For seafood entree, add spaghetti to boiling water and cook 2 to 3 minutes or until done.

Continued next page . . .

Hint

For a great fresh salad dressing, put chopped garlic, scallions, prepared mustard, olive oil, and balsamic vinegar in a small pitcher. As the liquid runs out, add more olive oil and vinegar and the chopped goodies will continue to flavor them.

10. Add crab, shrimp, Madeira, and wine to the mixture in frying pan. Reduce heat.
11. Slowly add the cream, salt, and pepper. When cream is warm, beat egg yolks with a small amount of sauce, then return the mixture to the pan. Add Italian tomato slices and heat, but do not boil.
12. Remove French bread from oven and slice.
13. For seafood entree, remove spaghetti from heat and drain in a large colander. Spoon seafood sauce on individual servings of spaghetti and serve immediately.

FOR ALL AGES

- Keep library books and board games in the living room, and use it as an inviting, peaceful haven for activities. Prioritize family pleasure and comfort over furniture care, and don't worry if the pristine appearance of your living room furniture isn't maintained.

- "Just say no" to your children occasionally, and don't be afraid to admit that you don't know everything.

- Give your children choices so they have input and ownership, but offer only a few choices—all of which you are prepared to accept.

- When you give your children money as a gift, always tell them to remember the Three S's: Spend Some, Share Some, and Save Some.

- Remember the importance of consistency in parenting. Never name consequences you are unwilling to carry out. As much as possible, make sure the consequences are related to the issue at hand and are never idle threats.

- Take the time to hug your kids every single day because way too soon you forget why you needed to be so efficient!

- Know that your children go through different stages and that your approach can modify as they grow and mature.

- Be a good model yourself, by doing social service in your community.

WEEK 6

Get Me to the Gym on Time

Daughter Julie played on the '94 Lakeside School girls basketball team that still holds the longest winning streak in Washington State girls basketball history—56 games spanning two seasons. During the long league season, we didn't have much time for dinner before the 7:30 P.M. tip-offs, so whatever I made had to be quick and easy. These tacos only take 15 minutes to prepare and can be eaten in even less time. I assume there will be more time for romantic, lingering dinners when the nest is empty!

Beef Tacos
with Fresh Orange Slices

Percentage of total
calories from the
following categories:

Protein: 25%
Carbohydrate: 40%
Fat: 35%

INGREDIENTS

1 tablespoon oil
1 pound lean ground beef
1 package taco sauce mix
1 tomato
½ head lettuce

¼ pound Cheddar cheese
1 ripe avocado
    taco shells
    light sour cream

FRUIT SIDE DISH

3 large oranges

1. For tacos, heat oil in a large saucepan over medium-high heat.
   Add lean ground beef and cook, stirring frequently, until done.
   Add sauce mix and prepare according to package directions.
2. Prepare taco condiments and place in a serving dish:
   • Chop the tomato in small chunks.
   • Shred the lettuce.
   • Grate the cheese.
   • Cut the avocado in chunks.
3. For fruit, cut both ends off of an orange with a sharp knife.
   Stand orange upright on a cutting board and, starting at the top,
   slice down and around the sides, just under the skin, until all
   skin is removed. Turn orange on its side and cut in ¼- to ½-inch-
   thick slices, then place on a serving dish. Repeat. Slices should
   look like pinwheels.
4. Heat taco shells in microwave for 1 minute on high.
5. Combine ingredients in a taco shell in order and amounts
   desired. Top with a dollop of light sour cream, if you wish.

Hint

Before you put
ground beef in the
freezer, place it in a
zip-lock freezer bag
and flatten the meat
with a rolling pin.
When you're ready to
use the beef, the
thin slab can easily
be cut into chunks
for quick browning.

WEEK 6

But, Officer ...

I was cooking dinner one Sunday evening when a phone call came from Colorado, where son Brad was spending his spring break with a college friend. The boys had arranged to stay in a condominium that belonged to the generous grandfather of a college classmate. A car, to be picked up at the airport, was also included in their friend's kind offer. The boys had been given car keys and vague instructions, but finally they located the late model Jeep in the airport parking lot. Off they went for four carefree days of skiing. Or so they thought.

Driving back to the condo after their second day on the slopes, they suddenly encountered a police roadblock. Officers approached the car, guns drawn, handcuffs ready. It seems the boys had "borrowed" the wrong car and the key, amazingly, had fit. Brad's phone call was coming from jail.

He sounded more calm than I felt, saying they had told the officers the truth and, once the facts were corroborated, were certain they would be released. As it turned out, that's exactly what happened within the hour. Their escapade made the Aspen newspaper the next day, and the real owner of the car was credited with "a good laugh and a free tank of gas" from the experience. All I gained were some unwanted gray hairs.

Brad called back the next evening and things were on the upturn. He wanted me to read him the following recipe over the phone. It seems a couple of girls they had met skiing were coming over.

Chicken Cashew with Rice
and Melon Slices

SERVES 4

Percentage of total calories from the following categories:

Protein: 17%
Carbohydrate: 58%
Fat: 25%

INGREDIENTS

3 cups raw rice	1 red bell pepper
4 boneless, skinned chicken breasts	1 10-ounce package frozen peas
½ onion	2 cloves garlic
2 large stalks celery	3 tablespoons oil
	½ cup dry-roasted cashews

MARINADE

1 tablespoon light soy	1 tablespoon cornstarch
1 tablespoon sherry	½ teaspoon each sugar and salt

SAUCE MIXTURE

¾ cup boiling water	2 teaspoons cornstarch
¾ teaspoon chicken bouillon	2 teaspoons light soy

FRUIT SIDE DISH

½ melon (cantaloupe, casaba, or honeydew)

1. For chicken entree, rinse rice and cook according to the directions on the package.
2. Slice chicken breasts in thin slices, then in 1-inch pieces.
3. Mix marinade ingredients in a mixing bowl and add chicken. Stir to coat chicken pieces completely.
4. Prepare vegetables:
   - Peel and quarter onion, then slice thinly.
   - Chop celery in fine pieces.
   - Slice red pepper in thin strips.
5. For fruit, slice melon and place on a serving plate.
6. For chicken entree, heat 1 tablespoon oil in a wide frying pan or wok over medium-high heat. Stir fry onions and celery for 1 to 2 minutes. Season lightly with half of sugar and salt. Remove from frying pan and set aside.
7. Add 1 tablespoon oil to wok and stir fry red pepper and peas for 1 to 2 minutes; season with remaining sugar and salt. Remove from pan and set aside.
8. Add remaining 1 tablespoon oil to wok and press garlic into pan.
9. Meanwhile, prepare sauce mixture of water, chicken bouillon, cornstarch, and light soy. When chicken is done, add sauce to wok, stirring until it thickens. Add vegetables and cashews.
10. Spoon chicken and vegetables over individual servings of rice and serve immediately.

Hint

To quickly slice a large onion, slice off the bottom and then make crossways cuts not quite through the onion, so that it still holds together. Turn the onion on its side and slice the other way and you'll have perfect dices.

WEEK 6

Week 6 Ingredients Lists

Parmesan Chicken with New Potatoes, Fresh Broccoli, and Green Salad

- ❑ 8 boneless, skinned chicken breasts
- ❑ 5 ounces grated Parmesan cheese
- ❑ ½ pint light sour cream
- ❑ lettuce or romaine
- ❑ 1 bunch green onions
- ❑ 6–8 red-skinned potatoes

- ❑ 1 large bunch broccoli
- ❑ 1 lemon

- ❑ butter or margarine
- ❑ dry bread crumbs
- ❑ garlic powder
- ❑ salad dressing
- ❑ whole black peppercorns

Indonesian Bami with Fruit Salad

- ❑ 1 pound flank steak
- ❑ 12 ounces dry spaghetti
- ❑ garlic
- ❑ 1 bunch green onions
- ❑ 1 small bunch celery
- ❑ 1 large leek
- ❑ ½ head cabbage

- ❑ 2 oranges
- ❑ 1 bunch grapes
- ❑ 1 small bunch bananas

- ❑ crushed red pepper
- ❑ soy sauce
- ❑ vegetable oil

Fisherman's Spaghetti with Green Salad and French Bread

- ❑ ¼ pound fresh baby shrimp
- ❑ 2 9-ounce packages fresh angel hair pasta
- ❑ 2 6-ounce cans lump crab meat (no leg meat)
- ❑ ½ pint half 'n' half
- ❑ lettuce or romaine
- ❑ 1 bunch green onions
- ❑ 3 Roma tomatoes
- ❑ 1 onion

- ❑ 8 mushrooms
- ❑ French bread

- ❑ butter or margarine
- ❑ 2 eggs
- ❑ Madeira
- ❑ oregano
- ❑ salad dressing
- ❑ white wine

Week 6 Ingredients Lists

Beef Tacos with Fresh Orange Slices

- [ ] 1 pound leanest ground beef
- [ ] 10-12 taco shells
- [ ] package taco sauce mix
- [ ] 3-4 ounces Cheddar cheese
- [ ] ½ pint light sour cream
- [ ] lettuce or romaine
- [ ] 1 tomato
- [ ] 1 avocado
- [ ] 3 oranges
- [ ] vegetable oil

Chicken Cashew with Rice and Melon Slices

- [ ] 4 boneless, skinned chicken breasts
- [ ] ½ cup dry-roasted cashews
- [ ] 10-ounce package frozen peas
- [ ] 1 head garlic
- [ ] 1 onion
- [ ] 1 red pepper
- [ ] 1 small bunch celery
- [ ] 1 cantaloupe, casaba, or honeydew melon
- [ ] chicken bouillon
- [ ] cornstarch
- [ ] light soy sauce
- [ ] raw rice
- [ ] sherry
- [ ] sugar
- [ ] vegetable oil

- [ ] 12   boneless, skinned chicken breasts
- [ ] 1   pound flank steak
- [ ] 1   pound leanest ground beef
- [ ] ¼   pound fresh baby shrimp

- [ ] 2   9-ounce packages fresh angel hair pasta
- [ ] 12   ounces dry spaghetti

- [ ] 5   ounces grated Parmesan cheese
- [ ] 2   6-ounce cans lump crab meat (no leg meat)
- [ ] 10–12   taco shells
- [ ] 1   package taco sauce mix
- [ ] 3–4   ounces Cheddar cheese
- [ ] ½   cup dry-roasted cashews
- [ ] ½   pint light sour cream
- [ ] ½   pint half 'n' half
- [ ] 1   10-ounce package frozen peas

- [ ] 1   head garlic
- [ ] 3   heads lettuce or romaine
- [ ] 2   bunches green onions
- [ ] 1   tomato
- [ ] 3   Roma tomatoes
- [ ] 2   onions
- [ ] 1   red pepper
- [ ] 6–8   red-skinned potatoes
- [ ] 8   mushrooms
- [ ] 1   large bunch broccoli
- [ ] 1   large leek
- [ ] ½   head cabbage
- [ ] 1   bunch celery
- [ ] 1   avocado
- [ ] 1   lemon
- [ ] 5   large oranges
- [ ] 1   bunch grapes
- [ ] 1   cantaloupe, casaba, or honeydew melon
- [ ] 1   bunch bananas

- [ ] 1   loaf French bread

Check:

- [ ] butter/margarine
- [ ] chicken bouillon
- [ ] cornstarch
- [ ] crushed red pepper
- [ ] dry bread crumbs
- [ ] eggs
- [ ] garlic powder
- [ ] light soy sauce
- [ ] Madeira
- [ ] oregano
- [ ] raw rice
- [ ] salad dressing
- [ ] salt and fresh ground black pepper
- [ ] sherry
- [ ] soy sauce
- [ ] sugar
- [ ] vegetable oil
- [ ] white wine
- [ ] whole black peppercorns

Week 7

Roast Chicken ✳
with Orzo Pilaf and Fruit Salad

❧

Greek-style Scampi ✳
with Couscous, Green Salad, and French Bread

❧

Country Spareribs ✳
with Spinach and Cornbread

❧

Chicken and Capellini Soup ?
with Pita Triangles and Cantaloupe Slices

❧

Turkey Sausage Risotto ?
with Green Salad and French Bread

Rams, Spam, Thank You, Man

Years ago, our family experienced the grandeur of Alaskan wilderness under the knowledgeable guidance of Keith Specking, a hunting and fishing expert and long-time patient of John's. Because the trek to his base camp was treacherous, Keith recommended we postpone our visit until Julie was at least 5 years old. So, two weeks after Julie's 5th birthday, we rolled up our sleeping bags, stuffed our duffels, armed ourselves with Jungle Juice to battle the mosquitoes, and headed to Alaska.

Certain memories are indelible: the vast expanses and scale of the state (Keith's wife, Vee, drives five hours for a haircut); the plentiful caribou, Dahl sheep, and mountain goats in Keith's backyard; a close-up view of a protective mother moose and her baby in Denali National Park; and little Julie clinging tightly to Keith's broad back as they crossed the rushing Brushkana River on horseback.

It was good for our citified kids to spend five days in such challenging, awe-inspiring surroundings. This was not a four-star wilderness experience with gourmet food, down comforters, and skylights in the cabin. We slept on the ground and our food was basic— Spam sandwiches for lunch and trout we had caught that afternoon for dinner. But in that awesome environment, even Spam tasted pretty good—just as I hope this Roast Chicken and Orzo Pilaf tasted to Keith and Vee when they came to Seattle.

Roast Chicken
with Orzo Pilaf and Fruit Salad

SERVES 4

Percentage of total calories from the following categories:

Protein: 32%
Carbohydrate: 37%
Fat: 31%

INGREDIENTS

3½–5 pound whole fryer roaster
    chicken
1 tablespoon butter or margarine

2 garlic cloves
salt and pepper

ORZO PILAF

½–1 large onion
3 medium tomatoes
¼ cup fresh basil leaves
2 tablespoons butter or
    margarine

2 large cloves garlic
1½ cups orzo
1 cup frozen peas
⅔ cup heavy cream
½ cup grated Parmesan cheese

FRUIT SALAD

small bunch grapes
1 banana

1 apple
2 oranges

1. Preheat oven to 350 degrees.
2. For orzo pilaf, fill a large pot with water and begin heating.
3. For chicken entree, wash chicken and place in a roasting pan. Dot skin with butter and rub with minced garlic, then season cavity with salt and pepper and sprinkle lightly on the skin. Place chicken in preheated oven and roast for 50 to 60 minutes or until done. Baste periodically.
4. For orzo pilaf, prepare ingredients:
   • Peel and quarter onion, then chop finely.
   • Cut tomatoes in half and squeeze to remove seeds, then chop.
   • Remove basil leaves from stems and cut coarsely.
5. Melt butter in a wide frying pan over medium heat. Press garlic into pan and add onion; cook for 5 to 7 minutes, stirring occasionally, until onion is soft but not brown.
6. Stir fresh tomatoes and basil into onion mixture. Reduce heat, cover, and simmer for 10 minutes.
7. Add orzo to water and cook about 10 minutes until tender to bite.
8. For fruit salad, prepare fruits and place in a bowl. Set aside.
9. For orzo pilaf, remove orzo from heat and drain well.

Continued next page . . .

Hint

Try roasting your chicken upside down so that the more abundant juices from the thigh drip down to flavor and tenderize the breast meat. This works great with your Thanksgiving turkey as well.

WEEK 7

10. Add peas and cream to tomato mixture. Increase heat to high and bring to a boil, then immediately stir in the cooked orzo. Remove from heat.

11. Stir grated Parmesan cheese into orzo mixture and add salt and pepper to taste. Sprinkle individual servings with more Parmesan, if desired.

12. Remove roast chicken from oven and cut into serving pieces. Serve immediately.

Advice

- An easy solution for kids who slam doors: after one or two warnings, simply remove the bedroom door from the hinges. It's easy to do and *very* effective!

- With kids' allowances, keep a chart in the kitchen and remember to subtract the money when some instant cash is needed. Keep a running total so they can see how much money they have left each week.

- You can bring an end to your adolescent's "gimme's" by putting a specified amount of money in a savings account every month that your child has to use for clothing, movies/entertainment, hair and skin care items . . . anything over and above the costs related to school and school activities/sports. The child can have his own debit card and must keep track of expenses incurred.

- As boys grow taller and pass Mom in stature . . . serious talks should always be conducted with Mom standing and the son sitting!

People Are People, Wherever . . .

With his engaging personality and enthusiasm, Mark Wen came to this country from Harbin, China, in 1988 to pursue his education. Mark currently heads a community college program developing educational relationships with Asian countries, but we met him through his work with Virginia Mason Medical Center's international department. In 1998, we traveled to Hong Kong, mainland China, and Taiwan with Mark. His knowledge of Chinese history, geography, art, and languages opened doors to fascinating cultures for us.

Mark is also an accomplished cook, and one night he invited himself to our house to cook dinner. First we visited an Asian market where we filled our basket with beef, pork, chicken, prawns, numerous vegetables from baby bok choy to Chinese cabbage, and some exotic spices. Back in my kitchen, Mark's hands flew preparing an amazing 10-course meal in an hour and a half. Every knife, pan, and serving dish I own needed to be washed, but it was an incredible feast. When it was my turn later to cook, it took me 35 minutes to produce just one entree. But Mark loved it.

Greek-style Scampi
with Couscous, Green Salad, and French Bread

SERVES 4

Percentage of total calories from the following categories:

Protein: 32%
Carbohydrate: 49%
Fat: 19%

INGREDIENTS

1¼ pounds large shrimp	1 tablespoon olive oil
2 28-ounce cans whole tomatoes	5 garlic cloves
½ cup fresh parsley	1 cup (4 ounces) feta cheese
2 tablespoons lemon juice	salt and freshly ground pepper

COUSCOUS

1½ cups water	¾ teaspoon salt
3 tablespoons butter or margarine	1½ cups couscous

GREEN SALAD

1 head lettuce or romaine
3–4 green onions
salad dressing

BREAD

1 loaf French bread

1. Preheat oven to 400 degrees.
2. For scampi, prepare ingredients:
   - Peel and devein shrimp.
   - Drain tomatoes, chop coarsely, and drain again.
   - Chop parsley.
   - Squeeze lemon juice.
3. Add olive oil to a large frying pan or Dutch oven over medium heat. Add garlic and saute for 30 seconds. Add tomatoes and ¼ cup parsley. Reduce heat and simmer 4 to 5 minutes.
4. Add shrimp to tomatoes and cook for 3 to 4 more minutes.
5. For couscous, combine water, butter, and salt in a large saucepan. Bring to a boil, then remove from heat and stir in dry couscous. Cover and let stand for at least 5 minutes. Fluff with a fork.
6. For scampi, pour shrimp and tomato mixture into a 9 x 13-inch baking dish and sprinkle with crumbled feta. Bake at 400 degrees for 10 minutes.
7. Place French bread on a cookie sheet and heat in warm oven.
8. For green salad, wash and dry lettuce or romaine, then chop and place in a salad bowl. Slice green onions, including tops, and add to salad bowl.
9. Add salad dressing and toss lightly. Serve on individual plates.
10. Remove French bread from oven and slice.
11. For scampi, remove shrimp and tomato mixture from oven and sprinkle with remaining ¼ cup parsley, lemon juice, salt, and pepper. Serve immediately.

Hint

Wash and spin dry lettuce or romaine as soon as you get home from the store. Lay a dish towel on the counter, put the lettuce on the towel, and tie up the opposite corners. Place in the "crisper" of your refrigerator and the lettuce will stay fresh for days.

A Troubling Truism

If optimism and a positive attitude could be measured, dear friends Penny and Paul Fredlund would be off the charts. Paul, an endocrinologist at Virginia Mason Medical Center, was once accused by the VMMC medical residents of suffering from an advanced case of "terminal euphoria." They're the kind of people who make you feel better just being in their presence.

But for all her good humor, Penny long ago passed along a keen observation that has stuck with me, particularly when I'm discouraged on behalf of one of my children. "A mother," she said, "is only as happy as her least happy child."

Unfortunate, but oh so true! And one more reason to work hard to maintain a supportive home environment. Hearty family dinners such as this can be part of that effort.

Country Spareribs

with Spinach and Cornbread

INGREDIENTS

6 large country-style pork
  spareribs
½ cup each sherry and water
½ onion
¼ lemon
1 teaspoon salt
⅛ teaspoon pepper

1 teaspoon chili powder
1 teaspoon celery seed
¼ cup Worcestershire sauce
1 cup ketchup
½ cup brown sugar
2 cups water

CORNBREAD

1 package cornbread mix   honey

VEGETABLE SIDE DISH

1 package frozen leaf spinach

1. For spareribs, prepare ingredients:
   • Peel and chop onion finely.
   • Slice lemon, including peel.
2. Brown spareribs in a large, flat frying pan over medium-high heat.
3. Add sherry and water to pan. Cover and lower heat to simmer, then cook spareribs for 2 hours.
4. Combine onion, lemon, salt, pepper, chili powder, celery seed, Worcestershire sauce, ketchup, brown sugar, and water in a saucepan. Bring to a low boil, then lower heat and simmer for 1½ to 2 hours.
5. Remove spareribs from heat and pour off liquid. Cover ribs with sauce and bake uncovered for 1½ to 2 hours at 300 degrees.
6. For cornbread, mix according to package directions and bake.
7. For vegetable, place frozen spinach in a microwave-proof dish and cook on high for 8 minutes. Remove spinach and drain. Butter lightly, then salt and pepper to taste.
8. Remove cornbread from oven. Cut in squares and serve with butter and honey, if desired.

SERVES 4

Percentage of total
calories from the
following categories:

Protein: 24%
Carbohydrate: 39%
Fat: 34%

Hint

Cut children's food with kitchen scissors—it's faster than a knife. This works on pizza and sandwiches and many foods you might not consider.

WEEK 7

Note: Cooking time for the spareribs totals 4 hours, but the first 2 hours can be done the morning of serving.

Relatively Speaking

Parental concern is #1, but children who enjoy the genuine interest of other adults in their lives are given a unique, affirming gift.

We are grateful our own kids have benefited from such relationships through a small group of close family friends. Although we're professionally diverse, we were drawn together by similar interests and values. Over the last 20 years we have shared childbirth, laughter, travel adventures, *Kum-ba-ya* and *Wild Thing*, sweaty sports and brain-testing games, political debates, wedding proposals, and even the agony of cancer.

Our kids are friends as well, and each has been enriched by the concern and thoughtful advice of the other parents, who help celebrate milestones, attend important events and games, write notes of encouragement and letters of recommendation, and even send care packages.

We've become so close we're nearly related. In fact, when then 3-year-old Andrew Stamm, the decided caboose among our collective ten kids, was told about an upcoming Christmas party, he wondered out loud, "Are all my relatives going to be there?" He meant us.

Friendships such as this require nurturing. So start this Saturday night and invite another family for dinner and games. Here's a simple meal suggestion.

Chicken and Capellini Soup
with Pita Triangles and Cantaloupe Slices

SERVES 4

Percentage of total
calories from the
following categories:

Protein: 34%
Carbohydrate: 46%
Fat: 20%

INGREDIENTS

4 boneless, skinned chicken breasts
1 small shallot
1 carrot
1 head Swiss chard
1 tomato
2 tablespoons butter or margarine
4 cloves garlic
½ teaspoon salt
¼ teaspoon dry thyme
2½ cups chicken broth
1½ cups water
½ cup dry white wine
6 ounces dry capellini, broken
    in half
grated Parmesan cheese

BREAD

1 package pita bread
   butter or margarine
grated Parmesan cheese

FRUIT SIDE DISH

½ cantaloupe

> **Hint**
>
> Double soup recipes
> and freeze in zip-lock
> bags. They lie flat in
> the freezer and thaw
> more quickly than a
> jarful of soup will.

1. Preheat oven to 350 degrees.
2. For soup, prepare ingredients:
   - Cut chicken into ½-inch chunks.
   - Finely chop shallot.
   - Peel carrot and slice thinly.
   - Trim Swiss chard and shred in thick ribbons.
   - Cut tomato in half, squeeze to remove seeds, and chop.
3. In a 3- to 4-quart pan or stockpot, melt butter over medium heat. Press garlic and add, along with shallots. Cook 2 to 3 minutes, stirring often, until shallot is soft.
4. Stir in chunks of chicken, salt, and thyme. Cook, stirring often, for about 3 minutes until chicken is done.
5. Add chicken broth, water, wine, and carrot slices. Bring to a boil over high heat, then reduce heat and simmer 10 to 15 minutes until carrot is tender.
6. For bread, cut pita rounds into fourths and tear apart the 2 layers. Spread the inside of each pita wedge with a small amount of soft butter and lay flat—butter side up—on a cookie sheet.

Continued next page . . .

WEEK 7

7. When all wedges are buttered, sprinkle lightly with grated Parmesan cheese and place in preheated oven. Bake for 10 minutes until golden brown.
8. For soup, add capellini to stockpot and bring to a boil. Cook, uncovered, stirring often, for 4 to 5 minutes, until pasta is al dente.
9. For fruit, remove rind from cantaloupe. Slice in wedges and place in a serving bowl.
10. For soup, add Swiss chard and tomato. Cover stockpot and remove from heat; let stand 2 minutes, just until tomato is heated through.
11. Sprinkle individual portions with Parmesan cheese.

WEEK 7

FOR MIDDLE ONES

- One mom from a big family with many cousins, aunts, and uncles, kept a master calendar with birthdays and holidays noted on it. At the appropriate time she put cards out on the counter for all three of her boys to write a note on, even when they were very small. As the boys grew, the notes did too, along with their thoughtfulness.

- To avoid squirminess and dissension on long car trips, make seat assignments: (1) front passenger is the navigator and determines the radio channel or music selection; (2) back seat #1 chooses where and when to stop for food; and (3) back seat #2 is in charge of car games and/or entertainment.

- Frame some of your child's art as if it were Picasso's—because to you it is. Let your child sign and title it. These works can even be hung proudly in inconspicuous places like the playroom or laundry room.

- Here's a good policy to initiate at a reasonable age: thank-you notes must be written before birthday/Christmas checks are cashed or out-of-town gifts worn or used.

- Everybody enjoys a surprise "theme" dinner. Celebrate your child's first harvest of lettuce with a "green" dinner. Cinco de Mayo is reason enough to serve tacos, or add blue jello and fishy crackers to a clam chowder menu after a day at the beach. Save brochures and ticket stubs from a vacation for a memory dinner once photos are developed. Any change or surprise sparks conversation, fun, and your child's imagination . . . it needn't be elaborate. A few chocolate coins to celebrate a child opening a new bank account will do the trick.

Secret Source

I think Brad surprised himself—and certainly John and me—when he developed an interest in cooking after he graduated from college. In the equal-opportunity households of today's young couples, this skill is a definite plus, even though many young men might rather be recognized for other talents.

When Brad tried the following risotto after reading about it in the local evening newspaper, he loved it. But his recommendation came with a somewhat anxious disclaimer. *"Please,"* he begged, "don't tell anybody who gave you this recipe!"

Whatever the source, this risotto is hearty, healthy, and easy to prepare.

Turkey Sausage Risotto
with Green Salad and French Bread

SERVES 4

Percentage of total
calories from the
following categories:

Protein: 27%
Carbohydrate: 40%
Fat: 33%

INGREDIENTS

½ large onion
8 ounces smoked turkey sausage
1 49½-ounce can chicken broth
  (6 cups)
1 tablespoon butter or margarine
1 tablespoon olive oil

3 cloves garlic
2 cups Arborio rice
½ cup sun-dried tomato
  halves, packed in oil
⅓ cup parsley leaves

GREEN SALAD

1 head lettuce or romaine
2.3-4 green onions

salad dressing

BREAD

1 loaf French bread

1. Preheat oven to 350 degrees.
2. For risotto, prepare ingredients:
   - Peel and quarter onion, then chop finely.
   - Slice turkey sausage in thin rings.
3. Pour chicken broth into a saucepan and heat on medium; keep warm.
4. In a large pot or Dutch oven, heat the butter and olive oil over medium heat. When hot, press the garlic into the pan and add onion; saute 5 minutes. Add the sliced sausage and the rice, and continue cooking for 5 minutes.
5. Meanwhile, in a food processor, combine the tomato halves, parsley, and 1 tablespoon of the oil in which tomatoes were packed. Process until finely chopped and set aside.
6. Begin to add the warm broth to the rice mixture, approximately 1 cup at a time, reserving ¼ cup broth. Cover and cook 4 minutes after each addition, until all broth is absorbed.
7. When last cup of broth is added, uncover pot and cook 15 minutes longer, or until rice is soft.
8. For green salad, wash and dry lettuce or romaine, then chop and place in a salad bowl. Slice green onions, including tops, and add to salad bowl.
9. Place French bread on a cookie sheet and heat in warm oven.
10. To complete green salad, add dressing and toss lightly. Serve on individual plates.
11. Slice French bread and serve immediately.

WEEK 7

Week 7 Ingredients Lists

Roast Chicken with Orzo Pilaf and Fruit Salad

- [ ] 3½–5 pound whole fryer roaster chicken
- [ ] 5 ounces grated Parmesan cheese
- [ ] ½ pint heavy cream
- [ ] 16-ounce package dry orzo pasta
- [ ] 10-ounce package frozen peas
- [ ] 1 head garlic
- [ ] ¼ cup fresh basil

- [ ] 3 tomatoes
- [ ] 1 large onion
- [ ] small bunch grapes
- [ ] 1 small bunch bananas
- [ ] apple
- [ ] 2 oranges

- [ ] butter or margarine

Greek-style Scampi with Couscous, Green Salad, and French Bread

- [ ] 1¼ pounds large shrimp
- [ ] 16-ounce package couscous
- [ ] 4 ounces feta cheese
- [ ] 2 28-ounce cans whole tomatoes
- [ ] 1 head garlic
- [ ] parsley
- [ ] lettuce or romaine

- [ ] 1 bunch green onion
- [ ] lemon
- [ ] French bread

- [ ] butter or margarine
- [ ] olive oil
- [ ] salad dressing

Country Spareribs with Spinach and Cornbread

- [ ] 6 large country-style pork spareribs
- [ ] package cornbread mix
- [ ] 10-ounce package frozen spinach
- [ ] 1 large onion
- [ ] 1 lemon

- [ ] brown sugar
- [ ] celery seed
- [ ] chili powder
- [ ] honey
- [ ] ketchup
- [ ] sherry
- [ ] Worcestershire sauce

Week 7 Ingredients Lists

Chicken and Capellini Soup
with Pita Triangles and Cantaloupe Slices

- ❑ 4 boneless, skinned chicken breasts
- ❑ 6 ounces dry capellini
- ❑ 5 ounces grated Parmesan cheese
- ❑ 2 14½-ounce cans chicken broth
- ❑ 1 head garlic
- ❑ 4 tomatoes

- ❑ 1 head Swiss chard
- ❑ 1 carrot
- ❑ 1 small shallot
- ❑ ½ cantaloupe
- ❑ 1 package pita bread

- ❑ butter or margarine
- ❑ thyme
- ❑ white wine

Turkey Sausage Risotto with Green Salad and French Bread

- ❑ 8 ounces smoked turkey sausage
- ❑ 16-ounce package Arborio rice
- ❑ 1 49½ can chicken broth
- ❑ 8.5-ounce jar sun-dried tomatoes, packed in oil
- ❑ 1 onion
- ❑ 1 head garlic
- ❑ parsley

- ❑ lettuce or romaine
- ❑ 1 bunch green onions
- ❑ French bread

- ❑ butter or margarine
- ❑ olive oil
- ❑ salad dressing

Week 7 Groceries

- [ ] 3½–5 pound whole fryer roaster chicken
- [ ] 6 large country-style pork spareribs
- [ ] 4 boneless, skinned chicken breasts
- [ ] 8 ounces smoked turkey sausage
- [ ] 1¼ pounds large shrimp

- [ ] 1 16-ounce package dry orzo pasta
- [ ] 6 ounces dry capellini
- [ ] 1 16-ounce package Arborio rice
- [ ] 1 16-ounce package couscous
- [ ] 1 package cornbread mix

- [ ] 5 ounces grated Parmesan cheese
- [ ] 4 ounces feta cheese
- [ ] ½ pint heavy cream

- [ ] 1 49½-ounce can chicken broth
- [ ] 2 28-ounce cans whole tomatoes
- [ ] 1 10-ounce package frozen peas
- [ ] 1 10-ounce package frozen spinach
- [ ] 1 8.5-ounce jar sun-dried tomatoes, packed in oil

- [ ] 2 large onions
- [ ] 1 small shallot
- [ ] 2 heads garlic
- [ ] ¼ cup fresh basil
- [ ] 4 tomatoes
- [ ] 1 head Swiss chard
- [ ] 1 carrot
- [ ] 1 bunch parsley
- [ ] 2 heads lettuce or romaine
- [ ] 1 large bunch green onions
- [ ] 1 small bunch grapes
- [ ] 1 banana
- [ ] 1 apple
- [ ] 2 oranges
- [ ] ½ cantaloupe

- [ ]   2   lemons

- [ ]   1   package pita bread
- [ ]   1   loaf French bread

Check:

- [ ] brown sugar
- [ ] butter/margarine
- [ ] celery seed
- [ ] chili powder
- [ ] honey
- [ ] ketchup
- [ ] olive oil
- [ ] salad dressing
- [ ] salt and fresh ground black pepper
- [ ] sherry
- [ ] thyme
- [ ] white wine
- [ ] Worcestershire sauce

Week 8

Garlic Beef with Green Beans ✳
and Fresh Orange Slices

Halibut with Roasted Vegetables, ⁊
Black Bean Mango Salsa, and Merry Bread

Herbed Pork Tenderloin
with Pat's Wild Rice Pilaf and Asparagus Spears

Prawns in Tomato Cream with Linguini
Green Salad, and French Bread

Chicken Pasta Michel
with Green Salad and French Bread

Every once in a while it's time to pull out the gastronomic stops. Is your mother-in-law visiting for the week? Is your old college buddy in town for a business conference and staying with you? Are you preparing the dinner to celebrate a birthday, graduation, or holiday?

If you want a week of great eating, with less concern about preparation time and calories, WEEK 8 is for you! There is a grocery list for this week, but you may just want to use the recipes on an individual basis for special occasions when you want to offer your family and friends an extraordinary meal. These recipes are perfect for company or for a special dinner for your own family —but for obvious reasons nutritional information is purposely not included. Just enjoy!

Breaking Out in a Rash

Friendly, intensely competitive, and a born motivator, Brad's best friend Ryan Kombrink was frequently at our house during high school. Here he and Brad religiously watched ESPN and pored over the agate-type sports stats. The boys met as teammates, but soon became soulmates and later roommates on a post-college basketball adventure to Denmark, where Ryan coached and Brad played professionally. Ryan fell in love with a Danish girl and is still in Copenhagen, moving right up in the Danish national coaching ranks. Brad, whose hang time is unfortunately less than Jordanesque, loved his brief moment in the spotlight but returned home to a "real" job.

Ryan was with us for many family dinners during those high school years, but he was somewhat difficult to cook for because of a self-imposed, color-coded food allergy. "I can't," he claimed, "eat anything green." Somehow this Garlic Beef with Green Beans met his approval and, not surprisingly, caused no allergic reaction.

Garlic Beef with Green Beans
and Fresh Orange Slices

INGREDIENTS

1 pound green beans	1 16-ounce package Marco Polo
2 bunches green onion	Chinese noodles
1½ pound flank steak	2 tablespoons vegetable oil
3–4 shiitake mushrooms	2¼ cups chicken broth
1 tablespoon minced, peeled	½ cup light soy sauce
fresh ginger	2½ tablespoons cornstarch
12 cloves garlic	3 tablespoons mirin
1 tablespoon sugar	1½ teaspoons sugar
2 tablespoons soy sauce	1 tablespoon sesame oil
1½ tablespoons mirin	¼ teaspoons pepper
(sweet rice wine)	

FRUIT SIDE DISH

3 large navel oranges

1. For garlic beef entree, prepare ingredients:
   * Trim green beans and cut in 3-inch slices.
   * Trim green onion and cut in ½-inch slices (including tops).
   * Slice flank steak very thinly and cut strips in half.
   * Slice shiitake mushrooms.
   * Peel fresh ginger and mince.
   * Trim and peel garlic.
2. Mix sugar, soy sauce, mirin, and 6 pressed garlic cloves thoroughly. Add flank steak slices to marinade.
3. Bring 4 quarts water to boil in a large pot, add green beans, and cook 5 minutes or until tender. Remove beans with a slotted spoon.
4. Add Chinese noodles to bean water. Cook until done and drain, then rinse under cold water and set aside.
5. Add 1 tablespoon vegetable oil to wok over medium-high heat. Add marinated flank steak, and stir fry 5 minutes or until browned but slightly pink in the center.
6. Combine chicken broth, light soy sauce, cornstarch, mirin, sugar, sesame oil, and pepper in a bowl. Stir well and set aside.

Continued next page . . .

Hint

Fresh ginger root stores well in the freezer. You can grate it while it's frozen and put the rest back in the freezer.

7. For fruit, cut both ends off of an orange with a sharp knife. Stand orange upright on a cutting board and, starting at the top, slice down and around the sides, just under the skin, until all skin is removed. Turn orange on its side and cut in ¼- to ½-inch slices, then place on a serving dish. Repeat. Slices should look like pinwheels.

8. For garlic beef entree, add 1 tablespoon vegetable oil to wok and stir fry mushrooms, green onions, ginger, and garlic.

9. Add broth mixture and bring to a boil. Cook 1 minute, stirring constantly, then add steak, green beans, and Chinese noodles. Stir fry 1 minute and serve immediately.

MISCELLANEOUS

- Always check smoke detectors January 1 and July 1.

- Tiny little bottlebrushes work well for cleaning dust out of computer keyboards.

- Remember to use the public library with its wealth of information on gardening, cooking, starting a business, publishing a book, parenting, etc. You can check out magazines from the library rather than subscribing to them. Such an inexpensive way to garner information!

- When you finally get to the store to buy a wedding/shower/birthday gift, buy an extra to put in the closet for those last minute occasions when you need a gift.

- Carry a bottle of water with you everywhere—to meetings, on planes, in cars, etc. Cover it with a sock from your "disappearing sock machine" (the dryer) so condensation won't dampen whatever the bottle touches.

- Wrap Christmas tree lights around a rolled-up newspaper to keep them tangle-free.

- You can save valuable seconds by loading the dishwasher with all the forks together, all the knives together, etc. When unloading, just grab the handful of forks and toss them into their slot in the silverware drawer.

With Friends Like This ...

The Weekly Feeder has been a few years in the making, and various people have added their wisdom—and sometimes a dose of sarcasm—to the writing process. One impromptu dinner with old friends Bob and Sandy Gannan ended in a comical discussion of potential Weekly Feeder sequels. Bob—who later called me on his car phone while stuck in traffic to discuss alternative book titles (Plan to Eat)—suggested that in my golden years I could write a series of sequels with recipes altered for gastrointestinal disorders common to senior citizens. The finale would be a book for octogenarians on Foods That Can Be Gummed. Maybe you had to be there.

Halibut with Roasted Vegetables
Black Bean Mango Salsa and Merry Bread

INGREDIENTS

4 1-inch-thick halibut steaks
1 teaspoon thyme
2 large sweet onions
2 red bell peppers
1 yellow bell pepper

salt and pepper
2 tablespoons orange zest
2 tablespoons olive oil
2 garlic cloves
salt and pepper

MARINADE

½ cup lime juice
¼ cup olive oil

¼ teaspoon pepper

MANGO SALSA

1 large ripe mango
1 large papaya
½ cup red onion
¼ cup fresh cilantro
2 tablespoons fresh lime juice
1 15½-ounce can black beans
2 garlic cloves

1 cup pineapple tidbits
1 teaspoon habanero pepper
   sauce
3 tablespoons olive oil
½ teaspoon ground cumin
   black pepper

BREAD

1 large loaf of dense, crusty
   peasant bread
1 cube butter
¼ cup grated Parmesan cheese

1 teaspoon seasoning salt
   (Johnny's Dock)
1 large clove garlic

1. Preheat oven to 375 degrees.
2. For halibut marinade, combine lime juice, olive oil, and pepper in a large, non-reactive flat baking pan. Add halibut steaks and turn to coat both sides. Cover and marinate 30 minutes.
3. For salsa, prepare ingredients:
   - Peel and cube mango.
   - Peel and dice papaya.
   - Peel and quarter red onion, then dice finely.
   - Mince fresh cilantro.
   - Squeeze fresh lime juice.
   - Rinse and drain black beans.
   - Mince garlic cloves.
   - Drain pineapple tidbits.

Continued next page . . .

> ### Hint
> Don't marinate vegetables before roasting or grilling because the acid in the marinade will make the vegetables too soggy.

WEEK 8

Halibut with Roasted Vegetables

CONTINUED . . .

4. Combine preceding salsa ingredients with pepper sauce, olive oil, cumin, and black pepper in a large bowl. Toss gently to coat and place bowl in refrigerator.

5. For halibut entree, prepare vegetables:
   - Peel and quarter onions, then slice thickly.
   - Cut red and yellow peppers into ¼-inch strips.
   - Remove zest from orange and cut in slivers.

6. Place onions, red and yellow peppers, and slivers of orange zest in a large, flat baking dish. Toss to coat with 2 tablespoons olive oil. Bake until vegetables start to brown and caramelize, stirring occasionally, about 20 minutes.

7. For bread, slice loaf horizontally and lay both halves, crust-side-down, on a large cookie sheet.

8. Soften butter briefly in microwave. Then add grated Parmesan cheese, seasoning salt, and minced garlic, stirring until mixture forms a smooth paste. Spread both halves of bread with this butter/cheese mixture and set aside.

9. For halibut entree, press garlic into vegetables and push vegetables to side of baking dish. Remove fish from marinade, pat dry, and place in center of baking dish. Sprinkle fish with thyme. Spoon vegetables on top of fish and bake until fish is opaque in center, about 10 minutes. Do not overcook. Salt and pepper to taste and serve.

10. Place bread in oven and bake for approximately 7 to 10 minutes, until toasty and golden. Remove from oven, slice, and serve immediately.

WEEK 8

MISCELLANEOUS

- If you're not ready to clean paintbrushes used with oil-based paint, wrap the paintbrushes in plastic wrap and store in the freezer for a day or two.

- Keep Band-Aids™ in your wallet or purse. It's amazing how often they come in handy!

- Organize videos in drawers so special family memories aren't taped over.

- When you make a long list of what to accomplish in a day, don't set yourself up for failure by creating an impossibly long and unrealistic list. Put the most difficult or time-consuming items at the top. Attack them early in the day, knowing that the next in line can be on the top of tomorrow's list.

Tokyo Roses

When you've spent your adult life working and raising a family in one community, a move can be difficult—particularly a move to a foreign country where language and cultural differences can be daunting.

But when friends Pat and Jim Fitzgerald were transferred to Tokyo for five years, they were determined to make the most of the experience. Pat's frequent emails tell tales of traditional tea ceremonies and typhoons, of the Sapporo Olympics and riding crowded subways to shop for a few groceries, of 5:00 A.M. Japanese language classes and the inflated cost of a round of golf. Pat's messages are typically upbeat, but once in a while she longs for something we take for granted. A recent message poignantly observed that with Tokyo's dense skyscrapers, flashing neon, and tangle of overhead freeways, she rarely sees the moon and never sees a sunset. Other than her roses, the thing Pat misses most of all is a simple view of the sky.

Pat is a superb cook, and I'm sure she's developing a wonderful repertoire of Japanese dishes. This Herbed Pork Tenderloin, however, is one of her old standbys and one of our favorite company dinners as well.

Herbed Pork Tenderloin
with Pat's Wild Rice Pilaf and Asparagus Spears

Hint
When entertaining, record the menu/wine/beverages you serve to avoid re-serving a meal to the same guests.

INGREDIENTS

2 large pork tenderloins
¼ cup light mayonnaise

1 teaspoon Dijon mustard

MARINADE

3 tablespoons olive oil
2 tablespoons lemon juice
2 teaspoons thyme

2 cloves garlic
1 tablespoon soy sauce

WILD RICE PILAF

½ cup wild rice
3 6 green onions
3 6 mushrooms
⅓ cup butter or margarine

½ cup currants
½ cup chopped ~~walnuts~~ pecans
1 tablespoon Worcestershire sauce
salt and pepper

VEGETABLE SIDE DISH

fresh asparagus

1. For pork entree, mix together olive oil, lemon juice, thyme, pressed garlic, and soy sauce in a small bowl, the night before serving.
2. Then, place pork tenderloins side by side in a large glass baking dish, prick on both sides with a fork, and pour marinade over tenderloins. Rotate during the day, allowing meat to soak up the marinade.
3. Preheat oven to 350 degrees.
4. For rice pilaf, pour chicken broth into a large saucepan and bring to a boil over high heat. Pour brown rice and wild rice into saucepan, cover, and lower heat to simmer. Cook rice for 1 hour or until done.
5. For pork entree, place tenderloins in oven and bake for 45 minutes or until barely pink.
6. For rice pilaf, prepare ingredients:
   • Slice green onions, including tops (approximately 1 cup).
   • Slice mushrooms (approximately 1 cup).

Continued next page . . .

Herbed Pork Tenderloin

CONTINUED . . .

7. For vegetable, wash asparagus carefully and trim off tough portion of stalk.
8. For rice pilaf, melt butter in a small skillet. Add green onions, mushrooms, currants, Worcestershire sauce, and walnuts.
9. For pork entree, mix together mayonnaise and Dijon mustard. Set aside.
10. For vegetable, place about 2 inches of water in a large pan and bring to a simmer. Cook asparagus until tender but not limp (between 30 seconds and 3 minutes, depending on size of asparagus). Remove from water and drain on paper towels. Season with salt and pepper.
11. Complete rice pilaf by adding hot rice to vegetables and tossing thoroughly. Season with salt and pepper.
12. Remove pork from oven and slice in ¼- to ½-inch slices. Serve immediately with a dollop of Dijon sauce.

Advice

KEEPING TRACK

- How many times have you forgotten to take something you need with you when you leave the house? Put your car keys with the item you need to take, so you can't leave without remembering it. You've made a dessert to take to a dinner party at your friends'? Put your car keys in the refrigerator right next to the dessert.

- When you're grocery shopping and have almost run out of checks, toss the check register in with the groceries. When you're unloading at home, you'll be "reminded" to put the next set of checks back in the checkbook, along with the register.

KEEPING UP WITH FRIENDS

- Along with a small packet of stamps, always keep a variety of greeting cards for various occasions, or a box of blank cards with neutral scenes like landscapes, florals, pets, etc., on hand to use for birthdays, thank yous, get well wishes, sympathy, etc. Write your own message or verse—it's much more personal that way.

- Keep postcards in your purse to keep in touch with out-of-town friends while waiting in line, stuck in traffic, or sitting at the doctor's office.

Put Away That Calorie Counter

My dad is quite trim and fairly active for his nearly 80 years. Daddy is usually served a heart-healthy diet by my very health-conscious mother, despite his not-so-secret fondness for butter on his bread, whole milk in his glass, half 'n' half on his cereal, and any dessert made with real whipped cream. One of our favorite photos of him shows him grinning from ear to ear as he stands in front of an all-you-can-eat dessert bar laden with exquisitely rich cakes, pies, and tortes. My dad has been a wonderfully generous grandpa, first as a willing babysitter and later as a dispenser of wise advice and an occasional financial boost to his three lucky grandkids. He has been so generous, in fact, that we all want to spoil him when he visits, by serving meals where calories and cholesterol aren't even mentioned.

This is an entree my dad particularly loves. I'm afraid it wouldn't taste the same made with nonfat milk.

Prawns in Tomato Cream with Linguini
Green Salad and French Bread

INGREDIENTS

⅓ cup sun-dried tomatoes
1 pound large shrimp
2 · 4 green onions
¼ cup chopped parsley
2 tablespoons oil
2 cloves garlic
1 cup heavy cream

¾ cup chicken broth
½ cup vermouth
1 tablespoon tomato paste
1 teaspoon dried basil
2 9-ounce packages linguini
½ cup feta cheese

GREEN SALAD

1 head lettuce or romaine
2 · 3-4 green onions

salad dressing

BREAD

1 loaf French bread

1. Preheat oven to 350 degrees and fill a large pot with water and begin heating.
2. For seafood entree, place sun-dried tomatoes in a small saucepan of boiling water and soften for 1 minute. Remove and drain.
3. Prepare ingredients:
   • Peel and devein shrimp.
   • Chop green onions, including tops.
   • Chop parsley.
   • Slice softened sun-dried tomatoes into slivers.
4. For green salad, wash and dry lettuce or romaine, then chop and place in a salad bowl. Slice green onions, including tops, and add to salad bowl.
5. For seafood entree, heat oil in a large skillet over medium-high heat. Saute shrimp, green onion, and garlic for 2 minutes. Transfer to a separate dish, cover with foil, and set aside. Reduce heat to medium.
6. Place French bread on a cookie sheet and heat in warm oven.
7. For seafood entree, add cream, chicken stock, vermouth, sun-dried tomatoes, tomato paste, and basil to the previously used skillet. Cook 5 to 7 minutes at a rolling boil until reduced and thickened.

Continued next page . . .

Hint

Do you sometimes forget to turn the oven off when you sit down to enjoy a meal? Try tying a brightly-colored ribbon made of fire-resistant fabric onto the oven door handle whenever the oven is in use, removing it once you have turned off the oven.

8. To complete green salad, add dressing and toss lightly. Serve on individual plates.
9. For seafood entree, add linguini to boiling water and cook 2 to 3 minutes until done. Drain well.
10. Return shrimp mixture to pan. Cook 2 to 3 minutes to heat through.
11. Slice French bread.
12. For seafood entree, transfer pasta to a large serving dish. Add sauce, feta cheese, and parsley. Toss well and serve immediately.

KEEPING CLEAN

- When polishing silver, use an old toothbrush to apply the polish to fork tines and around the cracks and curls of candlesticks, teapot handles, etc. Scrubbing with the bristles of a toothbrush gets at tarnish deep inside seams and around beaded designs, you-name-it.

- When you collect used towels from the bathrooms, use the slightly damp ones to quickly wipe the mirror, counter, and chrome fixtures and the bathroom looks "virtually" clean. It's a quick lift with almost no effort.

- Kitchen clean-up is a breeze if you can do the dinner preparation pots and pans as you go along. Or, if time is short and you have a double sink, fill the second sink with soapy water and keep putting your dirty prep bowls and utensils in there to soak. The dirty dishes are hidden until after dinner and your kitchen looks neat and clean as you cook.

- Cut up old t-shirts into squares to use for rags. Keep lots in a kitchen drawer as they're great for quick clean-up. Wash with bleach in the washing machine or just throw them away if they get too soiled.

Thank You, Karen!

I couldn't re-release *The Weekly Feeder* without acknowledging the contribution of Karen Michel, an Alaska mother of three teenagers and partner in her husband's construction firm. Karen bought the first edition of this cookbook and later over 30 extra copies for relatives, friends, co-workers, etc. She calls it "the standard Michel wedding gift." Along the way, she became a convert to the meal-planning system, and her heartfelt letter describing the book as a "lifeline when I was sinking" now sits framed on my desk. Karen felt guilty about her family's reliance on fast food and didn't have the confidence to entertain. Now her family is well fed, and Karen realizes that having guests can actually be fun.

So to Karen Michel—and anyone looking for a simple way to prepare and enjoy healthy, home-cooked meals—this one's for you!

Chicken Pasta Michel
with Green Salad and French Bread

INGREDIENTS

4 boneless skinned chicken
   breasts
   salt and pepper
14 Roma tomatoes
1 tablespoon olive oil
6 cloves garlic
1 red bell pepper
3 ~~6~~ green onions
½ cup sun-dried tomatoes,
   packed in oil

¼ cup chopped fresh basil
½ cup olive oil
1 tablespoon Dijon mustard
⅓ cup balsamic vinegar
1 teaspoon ground pepper
2 9-ounce packages fresh angel
   hair pasta or linguini
¾ cup Parmesan cheese
   salt and pepper

GREEN SALAD

1 head lettuce or romaine
2 ~~3-4~~ green onions

salad dressing

BREAD

1 loaf of French bread

1. Preheat oven to 375 degrees.
2. For chicken entree, place breasts in a lightly oiled glass baking dish. Season with salt and pepper to taste and bake in oven for 20 to 25 minutes or until barely done. Remove from oven.
3. Trim Roma tomatoes, slice in half lengthwise and place on a lightly oiled, rimmed cookie sheet. Brush lightly with olive oil, press garlic on top, and add salt and pepper to taste. Bake 20 minutes or until soft, and remove from oven.
4. Begin to heat water for pasta in a large pot.
5. Prepare other vegetables:
   - Chop red pepper into small squares.
   - Slice green onions, including tops.
   - Chop sun-dried tomatoes into small pieces.
   - Cut basil leaves into ¼-inch ribbons.
6. For green salad, wash and dry lettuce or romaine, then chop and place in a salad bowl. Slice green onions, including tops, and add to salad bowl.
7. For chicken entree, shred chicken using two forks to carefully separate strands.

Continued next page . . .

Hint

If you like to grate your own cheese, spray the grater with cooking spray and the cheese will shred cleanly without sticking to the grater.

WEEK 8

Chicken Pasta Michel

CONTINUED . . .

8. Coarsely chop roasted Roma tomatoes.
9. In a small bowl, mix together chopped sun-dried tomatoes, ½ cup olive oil, Dijon mustard, balsamic vinegar, pepper, chopped olives, and fresh basil.
10. Place French bread on a cookie sheet and heat in warm oven.
11. For chicken entree, place sauce mixture in a large saute or stir-fry pan over medium heat. Add red pepper and green onions. Cook over medium heat until vegetables are heated but still crisp. Add shredded chicken and chopped Roma tomatoes and heat through.
12. Meanwhile, add pasta to boiling water and cook until done. Drain well. Return to large pasta pot, and add sauce mixture with vegetables and chicken, and Parmesan cheese. Toss carefully.
13. To complete green salad, add dressing to greens and toss lightly. Serve on individual plates.
14. Slice French bread and serve immediately.

KEEPING NEAT

- To keep your home from looking cluttered, remember the phrase, "Don't put it down—put it away!" It only takes a second longer, but it makes a big difference!

- If your house is multi-story, make a pile of things to go up (or down) at the end of the day. You can leave things on one side of one of the stairs and take it all up at once, instead of making multiple trips. Laundry baskets make the pile easier to carry.

- Cleaning closets? Help others and save money on your tax bill by donating used clothing and other household goods to charitable organizations. Set up a master sheet with a list of clothing categories (men's shirts/women's skirts) and keep track of the number and fair market value of the items you give away so that you can report the donation at tax time.

- Empty toilet paper rolls are a great way to keep unruly electric cords in a drawer.

- Assign every child a kitchen drawer in which to store school photos, letters from Grandma, Halloween candy, knick-knacks, whatever they need a convenient place for. This clears a lot of clutter.

- Put plastic bags for wastebasket liners in the linen closet or close to where they will be used.

Week 8 Ingredients Lists

Garlic Beef with Green Beans and Fresh Orange Slices

- ❑ 1½ pound flank steak
- ❑ 16-ounce package Marco Polo noodles
- ❑ 2 14½-ounce cans chicken broth
- ❑ 1 pound fresh green beans
- ❑ 2 bunches green onion
- ❑ 1 large head garlic
- ❑ 3–4 shiitake mushrooms
- ❑ small chunk fresh ginger

- ❑ 3 navel oranges

- ❑ cornstarch
- ❑ light soy sauce
- ❑ mirin (sweet rice wine)
- ❑ sesame oil
- ❑ soy sauce
- ❑ sugar
- ❑ vegetable oil

Halibut with Roasted Vegetables, Black Bean Mango Salsa, and Merry Bread

- ❑ 4 inch-thick halibut steaks
- ❑ 5 ounces grated Parmesan cheese
- ❑ 15½-ounce can black beans
- ❑ 17-ounce can pineapple tidbits
- ❑ 2 large, sweet onions
- ❑ 2 red bell peppers
- ❑ 1 yellow bell pepper
- ❑ 1 head garlic
- ❑ 1 navel orange
- ❑ 3 limes
- ❑ 1 mango

- ❑ 1 large papaya
- ❑ 1 small red onion
- ❑ cilantro
- ❑ crusty peasant bread

- ❑ butter or margarine
- ❑ cumin
- ❑ habanero pepper sauce
- ❑ olive oil
- ❑ Johnny's Dock seasoning salt
- ❑ thyme

Week 8 Ingredients Lists

Herbed Pork Tenderloin
with Pat's Wild Rice Pilaf and Asparagus Spears

- ☐ 2 large pork tenderloins
- ☐ 8-ounce package wild rice
- ☐ 16-ounce package brown rice
- ☐ 14½-ounce can chicken broth
- ☐ 10-ounce package currants
- ☐ 3-ounce package chopped walnuts
- ☐ 1 bunch green onion
- ☐ 1 head garlic
- ☐ 6 mushrooms
- ☐ 1 lemon

- ☐ fresh asparagus

- ☐ butter or margarine
- ☐ Dijon mustard
- ☐ light mayonnaise
- ☐ soy sauce
- ☐ olive oil
- ☐ thyme
- ☐ Worcestershire sauce

Prawns in Tomato Cream with Linguini,
Green Salad, and French Bread

- ☐ 1 pound large shrimp
- ☐ 2 9-ounce packages fresh linguini
- ☐ 4 ounces feta cheese
- ☐ ½ pint heavy cream
- ☐ 6-ounce can tomato paste
- ☐ 14½-ounce can chicken broth
- ☐ 1 small bag sun-dried tomatoes
- ☐ parsley

- ☐ 1 bunch green onion
- ☐ 1 head garlic
- ☐ lettuce or romaine
- ☐ French bread

- ☐ basil
- ☐ salad dressing
- ☐ vegetable oil
- ☐ vermouth

Week 8 Ingredients Lists

Chicken Pasta Michel with Green Salad and French Bread

- ❑ 4 boneless, skinned chicken breasts
- ❑ 2 9-ounce packages fresh angel hair pasta
- ❑ 5 ounces grated Parmesan cheese
- ❑ 8.5-ounce jar sun-dried tomatoes packed in oil
- ❑ 14 Roma tomatoes
- ❑ 1 red bell pepper
- ❑ 1 head garlic

- ❑ 1 bunch green onion
- ❑ lettuce or romaine
- ❑ fresh basil
- ❑ French bread

- ❑ balsamic vinegar
- ❑ Dijon mustard
- ❑ olive oil
- ❑ salad dressing

- [ ] 1½   pound flank steak
- [ ] 1   pound large shrimp
- [ ] 4   boneless, skinned chicken breasts
- [ ] 4   inch-thick halibut steaks
- [ ] 2   large pork tenderloins

- [ ] 1   16-ounce package Marco Polo Chinese noodles
- [ ] 1   8-ounce package wild rice
- [ ] 1   16-ounce package brown rice
- [ ] 2   9-ounce packages fresh linguini
- [ ] 2   9-ounce packages fresh angel hair pasta

- [ ] 5   ounces grated Parmesan cheese
- [ ] 4   ounces feta cheese
- [ ] ½   pint heavy cream

- [ ] 1   6-ounce can tomato paste
- [ ] 3   14½-ounce cans chicken broth
- [ ] 1   15½-ounce can black beans
- [ ] 1   17-ounce can pineapple tidbits
- [ ] 1   10-ounce package currants
- [ ] 1   3-ounce package chopped walnuts
- [ ] 1   8.5-ounce jar sun-dried tomatoes, packed in oil
- [ ] 1   small bag sun-dried tomatoes (dry, in bag)

- [ ] 1   pound fresh green beans
- [ ] 2   large, sweet onions
- [ ] 14   Roma tomatoes
- [ ] 3   red bell peppers
- [ ] 1   yellow pepper
- [ ] 4   bunches green onions
- [ ] 3–4   shiitake mushrooms
- [ ] 1   small chunk fresh ginger
- [ ] 3   heads garlic
- [ ] 6   mushrooms
- [ ] 1   bunch parsley
- [ ] 2   heads lettuce or romaine

- ☐ ¼   cup fresh basil
- ☐ 4   large navel oranges
- ☐ 3   limes
- ☐ 1   lemon
- ☐ 1   large mango
- ☐ 1   large papaya
- ☐ 1   small red onion
- ☐ 1   bunch cilantro
- ☐ 1   large navel orange

- ☐ 1   loaf French bread
- ☐ 1   loaf crusty peasant bread

Check:

- ☐ balsamic vinegar
- ☐ basil
- ☐ butter/margarine
- ☐ cornstarch
- ☐ cumin
- ☐ Dijon mustard
- ☐ habanero pepper sauce
- ☐ light mayonnaise
- ☐ light soy sauce
- ☐ mirin (sweet rice wine)
- ☐ olive oil
- ☐ salad dressing
- ☐ salt and fresh ground pepper
- ☐ seasoning salt (Johnny's Dock)
- ☐ sesame oil
- ☐ soy sauce
- ☐ sugar
- ☐ thyme
- ☐ vegetable oil
- ☐ vermouth
- ☐ Worcestershire sauce

Desserts

I generally avoid temptation unless I can't resist it.

—MAE WEST

Just a Few (Drum Roll . . .) Desserts

It's time for a small confession. For over twelve years I have resolutely used this meal-planning system, grateful for its ease, consistency, and balanced nutrition. But deep down I've always regarded dinner as a brief pause on the way to the REAL main course . . . dessert!

I try to maintain some discretion at home and we usually end family meals with something simple like frozen yogurt or maybe a cookie or two. However, any company meal and all holidays are an opportunity to prepare a *real* dessert—butter, chocolate, sugar, and all.

Again, moderation is the key. A steady diet of rich sweets is obviously bad for your heart, your arteries, and your waistline. But if your regular diet is healthy, why not enjoy a decadent dessert every once in a while? With that philosophy in mind, I offer some of my favorites. There's nothing low fat, low calorie, or heart smart about any of them, but they are all very good. These are not staples . . . these are treats.

The first group of dessert recipes are cookies, mostly bar-type that are quick and easy to prepare and great to take to a potluck or serve to a casual group. Next, I've included a few fun breakfast specials for lazy Saturdays or special holidays. Then you'll discover a number of scrumptious, elegant edibles that are perfect for more formal company gatherings. The finale is the ultimate dessert—a cherished candy recipe shared by a dear friend. It's simply the best.

There's no system to these desserts, no organization, and definitely no nutritional analysis. But I couldn't write a cookbook without including them.

Hint

Sending cookies to kids away at college? Use fresh-popped popcorn as the packing material. The cookies will arrive whole, with an extra snack as a bonus!

Our favorites. These bars are durable enough for collegiate care packages, quick enough for last minute preparation, and use ingredients you may already have on hand. The milk chocolate chips are the secret ingredient.

Chocolate Chip Bars

INGREDIENTS

1½	sticks butter		2	large eggs
1	teaspoon salt		2¼	cups unsifted flour
1	teaspoon vanilla		1	teaspoon baking soda
¾	cup granulated sugar		1	teaspoon hot water
¾	cup brown sugar, firmly packed		12	ounces milk chocolate chips

Preheat oven to 375 degrees.

Cream butter in the large bowl of an electric mixer, and then add salt, vanilla, and both sugars. Beat well. Add the eggs and beat after each addition. On low speed, add half of the flour and beat only until incorporated. In a small cup stir the baking soda into the hot water to dissolve, then mix it into the dough. Add the remaining flour and beat only to mix. Remove the bowl from the mixer and stir in the chocolate chips.

Spread the dough in a 10 x 15-inch jelly roll pan and bake for 12 minutes or until lightly browned. Don't overcook—these are best if they're slightly chewy. Cool before cutting into bars.

Note: Spoonfuls of dough dropped on a cookie sheet and baked for 10 minutes are less chewy, but equally irresistible.

These bar cookies are more time-consuming to make, but the result is like a rich shortbread cookie drenched in thick caramel, and worth the extra effort.

Hint

If you don't bake very often, you may need to check the potency of baking powder that has been sitting in your cupboard. Simply mix 2 teaspoons of baking powder into a cup of water. If the mixture immediately foams and fizzes, the baking powder is fresh enough to use. If the reaction is weak or delayed, you should buy a new can.

Chocolate Caramel Cookies

FIRST LAYER

1	cup butter		2	cups flour
½	cup sugar		1	teaspoon baking powder

SECOND LAYER

1	cup butter		¼	cup light corn syrup
1	cup firmly packed brown sugar		1	14-ounce can sweetened condensed milk

THIRD LAYER

6 ounces semi-sweet chocolate

Preheat oven to 350 degrees.

For first layer, cream butter and sugar with an electric mixer, then gradually add flour and baking powder, beating well after each addition. Pat into a 9 x 13-inch baking pan. Bake for 15 to 20 minutes, or until lightly browned. Cool.

For second layer, melt butter, brown sugar, corn syrup, and sweetened condensed milk in a heavy saucepan. Bring to a boil and stir constantly for 8 minutes—to 238 degrees on a candy thermometer. Pour over first layer and cool.

For third layer, melt chocolate and immediately spread over caramel layer. Cool cookies until firm before cutting into squares.

If you love shortbread and nuts, these bars combine both with a honey glaze. They're a little sophisticated for young palates, but I served them once with a scoop of ice cream and a dab of fudge sauce. Mmmmm.

Pecan Squares

CRUST

1	cup butter, softened	2	cups flour
⅔	cup powdered sugar		

Preheat oven to 350 degrees.

Process ingredients in a food processor until crumbly and pat into a 9 x 13-inch baking pan. Bake for 20 minutes and remove from oven.

TOPPING

⅔	cup butter		
½	cup honey	½	cup brown sugar
3	tablespoons heavy cream	8	ounces chopped pecans

Melt butter and add honey, cream, and brown sugar. Stir in pecans, coating them thoroughly. Spread over crust. Return to oven and bake for another 20 minutes. Cool completely before cutting into squares.

These are a cross between cake and brownies, with a warm frosting that always dribbles over the top of the jelly roll pan and makes delicious chocolate puddles on the counter.

Duwamish Mud Bars

INGREDIENTS

1	cup butter	1	teaspoon baking soda
¼	cup unsweetened cocoa	1	teaspoon vanilla extract
1	cup water	2	cups sugar
2	eggs	2	cups flour
½	cup buttermilk	½	teaspoon salt

FROSTING

1	cup butter	1	pound powdered sugar
	pinch of salt	1	teaspoon vanilla
¼	cup unsweetened cocoa	¼	cup chopped nuts
6	tablespoons buttermilk		(optional)

Preheat oven to 350 degrees. Butter a 10 x 15 x 1-inch rimmed cookie sheet.

Over low heat, melt together butter, cocoa, and water. In the large bowl of an electric mixer, beat together eggs, buttermilk, baking soda and vanilla. Add butter/cocoa mixture to egg mixture. Slowly add sugar, then flour and salt. Pour into prepared pan and bake for 15 minutes.

While bars are baking, prepare frosting. Combine and cook butter, salt, cocoa, and buttermilk over medium heat. Remove pan from burner and add powdered sugar, vanilla, and nuts, if desired. Slowly pour hot topping over cake while cake is still hot, spreading with a spatula if necessary. Cut into bars while still warm. Cool before serving.

Hint

When making lemon cookies or pies, don't add the eggs to the lemon juice and let the mixture sit. The acidic lemon juice "cooks" the protein in the eggs and your pie or cookies will be runny. Mix them right before cooking.

Daughter Jill has enjoyed many exciting travel adventures with her friend Robin Wyman and Robin's family. Back home, we have always enjoyed Robin's mom's fabulous lemon bar recipe.

Polly's Lemon Squares

SHORTBREAD BASE

2	cups flour	1	cup melted butter
½	cup powdered sugar		

Preheat oven to 325 degrees.

Place dry ingredients in the bowl of a food processor and add melted butter through the feed tube. When thoroughly mixed, spread in a 9 x 13-inch baking pan and bake for 20 minutes.

TOPPING

4	eggs	¼	cup flour
⅓	cup fresh lemon juice	½	teaspoon baking powder
2	cups granulated sugar		

Beat eggs, lemon juice, and sugar in food processor until light. Add flour and baking powder. Pour over crust and bake for 20–25 minutes. Dust with powdered sugar. Cool thoroughly before cutting.

Here's another basic recipe from my mother-in-law's kitchen—and absolutely the best ammunition I've ever found for kids armed with cookie cutters. The dough is durable and delicious, perfect for those Halloween pumpkins, Christmas trees, and Valentine hearts.

Frosted Cookies

INGREDIENTS

½	cup butter or margarine	1	teaspoon soda
½	cup shortening	1	teaspoon vanilla
3	cups flour	2	eggs
1	teaspoon cream of tartar	1	cup sugar
1	teaspoon salt		

Cream butter and shortening. Slowly add flour and other dry ingredients except sugar. Add vanilla and eggs and mix well. Add sugar last; the dough will feel very grainy. Chill for 2 hours or more to make dough easier to handle.

Roll dough to approximately ¼-inch thickness. Cut with cookie cutters and bake cookies at 350 degrees for 8 minutes.

FROSTING

½	cup butter, softened		dash of milk
1½	cups powdered sugar	1	teaspoon vanilla

Beat together well. Add food coloring as desired.

Hint

Great idea for grandmas— with two or three friends, invite all your grandchildren under age 9 over to decorate holiday cookies. Bake the cookies in holiday shapes ahead of time, then put out frostings of every color, plus candies, etc., to decorate with. Cover the floor with tarps so you won't worry about the mess. Everyone will have a great time.

Hint

When you bake a batch of cookies, double the recipe but only bake part of the dough. Using a melon baller (or ice cream scoop if you have a serious sweet tooth), make dough balls and freeze them on a cookie sheet until firm, transferring balls later to a zip lock bag. If someone stops by, or you have a sudden craving for a treat, put a few in the oven and—voila!—fresh, hot cookies in just minutes.

An administration-assigned freshman roommate can sometimes be a disastrous match for a college student, but Julie hit the jackpot with Lauren Blaustein. With seemingly little in common (actress/athlete, reggae/rock, loves cats/loves dogs, etc.), the girls nevertheless built a long-lasting friendship and are now in San Francisco working in their first post-college jobs. They're still roommates—and still love to receive these cookies in the mail.

Double Chocolate Chippers

INGREDIENTS

1	cup granulated sugar	⅔	cup cocoa
1	cup brown sugar	1	teaspoon soda
1	cup butter or margarine	½	teaspoon salt
2	eggs	12	ounces white chocolate chips
2	cups flour		

Preheat oven to 350 degrees.

Cream together sugars, butter, and eggs. Blend in dry ingredients a small amount at a time, and carefully stir in white chocolate chips. Drop by spoonfuls on a cookie sheet and bake for approximately 10 minutes or until done.

These bars have an unusual brown sugar meringue that bakes to a toasty brown. The shortbread base is soft and rich.

Hint

Some people find it much faster to weigh ingredients that might be hard to measure, such as brown sugar or bulk chocolate chips— these foods are also much less expensive to purchase in bulk than the pre-packaged variety.

Chocolate Half 'n' Halfs

SHORTBREAD BASE

½	cup butter or margarine	2	cups flour
½	cup shortening	1	teaspoon baking powder
½	cup brown sugar	¼	teaspoon salt
½	cup granulated sugar	¼	teaspoon soda
2	eggs, separated	1	teaspoon vanilla
1	tablespoon water		

TOPPING

6	ounces chocolate chips	1	cup brown sugar

Preheat oven to 350 degrees.

Cream together butter, shortening, and sugars, then add egg yolks beaten with water. Slowly blend in dry ingredients and spread dough in a 9 x 13-inch pan. Cover shortbread with chocolate chips. Add 1 cup brown sugar to 2 egg whites and beat until stiff. Spread meringue over chocolate chips and bake for 20 to 25 minutes or until done. Cool before cutting in squares.

These dense, fudgy brownies only *appear* difficult to make. An artistic drizzle of chocolate looks elegant on the creamy white frosting with just a hint of mint, and makes the humble brownie an all-star.

Mint Brownies

INGREDIENTS

1	cup butter	2	cups sugar
4	ounces unsweetened chocolate	1	cup flour
4	eggs		

Preheat oven to 350 degrees.

Melt chocolate and butter together. Beat eggs and sugar until ivory-colored; add flour and chocolate-butter mixture. Bake in a 9 x 13-inch pan for 25 minutes. Cool in pan.

FROSTING

3	cups powdered sugar	¼	cup milk
6	tablespoons soft butter	¾	teaspoon peppermint extract

Mix frosting ingredients and spread over cooled brownies. Chill in refrigerator for ½ hour, then drizzle with swirls and dots of the following glaze. Cool before cutting. Brownies are best kept in the refrigerator.

GLAZE

½	ounce unsweetened chocolate	¼	cup powdered sugar hot water
½	teaspoon butter		

Melt chocolate and butter together. Add powdered sugar and thin with hot water until consistency of very thick syrup.

One night John volunteered to prepare the snack I had offered to bring to an early morning committee meeting. Enjoying a second slice the next day, my friend Marty Weiden observed that the dense, buttery coffee cake was "not only homemade, it was manmade."

It's another wonderful creation from Grandma Toots' recipe file.

Manmade Coffee Cake

INGREDIENTS

1	cup sugar	1	teaspoon vanilla
1½	sticks butter	3	cups flour
2	eggs	1	tablespoon baking powder
1	cup milk	½	teaspoon salt

Preheat oven to 350 degrees.

Cream sugar and butter with an electric mixer, then add eggs, milk, and vanilla. Beat until smooth. Slowly add the flour, baking powder, and salt. Spread half of the mixture in a 9 x 13-inch baking pan. Mix filling ingredients together and cover batter with half of the following filling, then add the rest of the batter and the remaining filling. Melt 6 tablespoons butter and drizzle over the top. Bake 30 minutes or until done.

FILLING

1	cup brown sugar	2	tablespoons cinnamon
2	tablespoons flour	1	cup nuts, if desired

Susan Blumenfeld, an old college friend, neighbor, and accomplished cook, gave me this recipe. Deceptively easy, it looks and tastes like it's straight from the neighborhood bakery.

Swedish Almond Roll

PASTRY BASE

1	cup flour	2	tablespoons water
1	stick butter, softened		

Mix ingredients together in a food processor until thick and pasty; divide in half. Smooth the halves on a cookie sheet in two parallel 3 x 12- to 15-inch rectangles.

TOP LAYER

1	stick butter	3	eggs
1	cup water	½	teaspoon almond extract
1	cup flour	¼	teaspoon salt

Preheat oven to 375 degrees.

Bring butter and water to a boil in a medium saucepan. Remove from heat and quickly add flour. Add eggs separately, beating well after each addition. Add almond extract and salt. Spread this mixture, which is like a paste, on top of the pastry layer. Bake for 40 minutes or until golden brown.

FROSTING

2	cups powdered sugar	2–3	tablespoons milk
¼	cup butter, softened	½	teaspoon almond extract

Beat ingredients well and frost almond rolls while still warm. Top with slivered or sliced almonds, if desired.

Another "Grandma Toots" special. Whenever we visit John's parents, our kids ask for these wonderful cinnamon biscuits for breakfast. She is always happy to oblige.

Angel Biscuits

INGREDIENTS

5	cups flour	1	cup shortening
¼	cup sugar	1	package dry yeast
1	tablespoon baking powder	¼	cup warm water
1	teaspoon soda	2	cups buttermilk

Place dry ingredients in a bowl and cut shortening in. Dissolve yeast in warm water and add to dry ingredients along with the buttermilk. Mix until all dry ingredients are moist. Roll half of the dough into a large rectangle, ⅜-inch thick and approximately 15 x 6 inches. Spread with half of the following mixture:

CINNAMON FILLING

½	cup butter or margarine	1¼	cups sugar
		1	tablespoon cinnamon

Preheat oven to 375 degrees.

Roll rectangle up lengthwise, and cut biscuits into ¾-inch slices. Place slices flat on a greased cookie sheet and bake for 15 minutes at 375 degrees or until done. Repeat with other half of the dough and the remaining cinnamon-sugar mixture.

Hint

Freeze butter in small chunks and use for crust made in a food processor. The mixture stays crumbly.

This tart also looks and taste like something you picked up at a local French bakery. No one will believe you made it yourself, and it's surprisingly easy.

Almond Tart

PASTRY

1½	cups flour	½	teaspoon salt
1	stick butter	1	egg

Preheat oven to 325 degrees.

Place all ingredients together in a food processor and process until dough leaves the side of the bowl. Press dough evenly over the bottom and sides of an 11-inch fluted tart pan with removable bottom. Bake for 10 minutes. Using the back of a spoon, very carefully smooth out any cracks that may appear in the pastry and would allow the filling to seep through.

FILLING

1½	cups whipping cream	½	teaspoon grated orange peel
1½	cups sugar	6	ounces sliced almonds
¼	teaspoon salt	1	teaspoon almond extract

Raise oven temperature to 375 degrees.

In a heavy 3-quart saucepan, combine whipping cream, sugar, salt, and orange peel. Bring to a boil, stirring occasionally. Reduce heat to simmer and cook 5 minutes. Remove from heat and stir in almonds and almond extract. Pour into pastry. Place tart on rack in the middle of oven and put an empty cookie sheet on the bottom rack to catch any drips. Bake at 375 degrees for 35 to 40 minutes, or until the top of the tart is a rich brown. Cool before slicing in wedges.

This Almond Torte is more cake-like than the Almond Tart, but for those of us who can never get enough of the rich flavor of almond, it's just as delicious.

Almond Torte

INGREDIENTS

1	cup butter	2	cups flour
4	ounces almond paste	1	egg, separated
⅓	cup sugar	½	cup sliced almonds
1	teaspoon almond extract		

Preheat oven to 350 degrees.

Cream butter and sugar together with an electric mixer, then add almond paste in small bits. Beat well after each addition. Add egg yolk and almond extract and mix thoroughly, then stir in flour a little bit at a time.

Line bottom of a 9-inch round cake pan with waxed paper. Do not grease. Press cake mixture evenly into pan.

Beat egg white until frothy but not stiff and spread over cake batter. Sprinkle almonds on top and bake for 30 minutes.

Cake is best if it sits uncovered for a day. Cut in wedges and serve.

Some guests from Singapore were so taken with this All-American dessert that giving them the recipe wasn't enough. At the end of our meal they politely asked me to demonstrate how to make Apple Crisp. Fortunately I had some extra apples, and they watched intently as I prepared a second crisp to send along with them.

Apple Crisp

FRUIT BASE

4	cups apples, peeled, quartered, and sliced thinly	¼	cup orange juice

TOPPING

1	cup sugar	1	heaping teaspoon cinnamon
¾	cup flour	6	tablespoons butter
½	teaspoon salt		

Preheat oven to 375 degrees.

Place sliced apples in a pie pan and drizzle with orange juice. Put remaining ingredients in a food processor and process until crumbly. Sprinkle on top of apple slices.

Bake for 30 to 35 minutes or until golden brown. This crisp is best served warm with vanilla ice cream or frozen yogurt.

As a bit of a fruit crisp connoisseur, I've tried many different recipes over the years. This is my current favorite.

Hint

Don't limit yourself to apple or berry crisps. Wonderful crisps and cobblers can be made from dark sweet and sour cherries, Italian plums, pears, apricots, peaches, nectarines, or even rhubarb.

Apple Berry Crisp

FRUIT BASE

6	apples, Golden Delicious or Granny Smith	½	cup sugar
		2	tablespoons flour
1	large bag frozen mixed berries		

TOPPING

1	cup rolled oats	½	cup butter
1	cup flour	⅔	cup brown sugar
½	cup chopped nuts (optional)	2	teaspoons cinnamon

Preheat oven to 350 degrees.

Peel, core, and quarter apples, then slice thinly. Place in a buttered 9 x 13-inch baking dish. Top with frozen mixed berries. Mix together sugar and flour and sprinkle over fruit.

Melt butter in a large glass bowl in the microwave, then add oats, flour, nuts, brown sugar, and cinnamon. Mix until crumbly and sprinkle topping over the filling.

Bake the fruit crisp for 35 to 40 minutes until fruit is soft and bubbly and topping is browned. Serve warm, topped with vanilla ice cream or frozen yogurt, or whipped cream.

With a buttery crust, rich cream filling, and colorful array of fruits, this is a gorgeous dessert. Experiment with your own favorite fruits in colorful combinations.

Fruit Tart

CRUST

½	cup butter	¼	teaspoon almond extract
¼	cup sugar	1	cup flour
6	tablespoons ground almonds		

Preheat oven to 350 degrees.

Cream butter and sugar in a food processor. Gradually add ground almonds, almond extract, and flour. Mix until dough is soft and smooth. Press into sides and bottom of an 11-inch fluted tart pan. Bake for 20 minutes. Cool crust completely before filling with Cream Patisserie.

CREAM PATISSERIE

4	egg yolks	¼	teaspoon salt
¾	cup sugar	1½	cups scalded milk
3	tablespoons flour	¼	teaspoon vanilla

Beat egg yolks and sugar until mixture is thick. Stir flour and salt into eggs. Slowly stir in hot milk and heat to boiling. Boil, stirring constantly, for 2 minutes on medium-low heat. Whisk cream for 2 to 3 minutes until cooled. Stir in vanilla. Sprinkle with a small amount of sugar or melted butter to prevent a "skin" from forming. Cover and refrigerate until chilled, and then spread cream in a tart shell. (Cream can also be frozen.)

Arrange the following fresh fruit on top, beginning at the outer edge:

- an overlapping row of very thinly sliced banana around the perimeter
- a wide ring of canned crushed pineapple
- a "flower" of mandarin oranges in the center, sprinkled with blueberries.

Just use your imagination!

This pie has been a family joke ever since I first tried the recipe nearly 25 years ago. John and I each had one piece, and I liked it so much I ate the entire remainder of the pie for breakfast the next morning. Orange marmalade and a crumb topping elevate this homely Thanksgiving regular to gourmet status. It's simply the best pumpkin pie I've ever tasted.

Hint

When making pie crust it's helpful to remember that different shortenings contain different amounts of water. If the dough isn't sticking together, just add a little more water.

Crumb-topped Pumpkin Custard Pie

9" unbaked pie shell

FILLING

2	eggs	1	cup evaporated milk
1½	cups pumpkin	¼	cup water
⅓	cup brown sugar	⅓	cup orange marmalade
1	teaspoon cinnamon		
¼	teaspoon each ginger, nutmeg, and salt		

Preheat oven to 350 degrees.

Beat eggs slightly, then stir in pumpkin, brown sugar, cinnamon, ginger, nutmeg, and salt. Blend in milk, water, and orange marmalade. Pour into pie shell and bake for 20 minutes.

Carefully remove pie from oven and sprinkle with the following topping, combined until crumbly. Bake 30 minutes longer.

TOPPING

½	cup graham cracker crumbs	½	teaspoon cinnamon
½	cup granulated sugar	3	tablespoons melted butter

Another holiday staple at our house. The bright red raspberries are perfect at Christmastime, but the torte tastes just as great in the summer when it's made with fresh berries.

Raspberry Torte

INGREDIENTS

1	10-ounce package quality shortbread cookies (like Pepperidge Farm)	1	egg
		1	teaspoon vanilla
		1	large bag frozen raspberries
6	tablespoons butter	½	pint heavy cream
2	cups powdered sugar		

Place cookies in a food processor and process until fine crumbs form. Place half of the cookie crumbs in the bottom of a 9 x 9-inch glass baking dish. Cream butter and sugar, then add egg and vanilla, mixing until smooth and glossy. Carefully spread over cookie crumbs, then place raspberries on top. Whip heavy cream until stiff and spread over the berries, then sprinkle with remaining cookie crumbs and refrigerate.

Not only does Patty Lakamp do everything well, she does it with a smile on her face. She was really grinning when she gave me this recipe.

Hint

If you bake a lot, it's helpful to have two mixer bowls, two food processor bowls, and two sets of measuring spoons and cups so you don't have to continually wash them while you're baking.

Chocolate Mousse Cake

INGREDIENTS

9	eggs, separated	3	1-ounce squares unsweetened chocolate
⅔	cup sugar		
4	cups heavy cream	2	tablespoons water
3	4-ounce packages German chocolate	1½	teaspoons vanilla
		2	packages ladyfingers

Cream egg yolks and sugar together in a big bowl using an electric mixer. In a separate bowl, beat egg whites until stiff and set aside. In a third bowl, whip all the heavy cream until soft peaks form and set aside.

Melt both chocolates together in the top of a double boiler over hot water and remove from heat. Stir in water and vanilla. Mixture will thicken.

Pour egg yolk and sugar mixture into the melted chocolate and mix until well blended, then fold in beaten egg whites. Add just less than half the whipped cream, reserving the rest.

Grease a 10-inch springform pan. Line the bottom and sides of the pan with ladyfingers, rounded side out. Tear the ladyfingers to fit the bottom of the pan—you may have some left over. Pour half of the chocolate mixture into the pan and top with half the remaining plain whipped cream. Pour the remainder of the chocolate mixture over the first whipped cream layer and top with the rest of the whipped cream.

Chill for several hours, preferably overnight.

There could be no more loyal friend than Nina Fogg, and there's simply no better homemade candy than her Chocolate Almond Toffee. The instructions are very specific, but not nearly as complicated as they appear. This spectacular candy is worth every single calorie!

Nina's Chocolate Almond Toffee

INGREDIENTS

1	pound whole almonds	2	cups sugar
1	3-ounce package sliced almonds	2	7-ounce bars Hershey's milk chocolate
1	pound butter		

Process whole almonds in a food processor on high for 15 to 17 seconds until almonds are coarsely chopped. Set aside.

Melt butter on low in a large, heavy saucepan. Before butter is totally melted, add sugar, increasing heat to medium high. Stir with a wooden spoon until bubbly, then add sliced almonds. Continue cooking, stirring gently, until candy thermometer reaches 297 degrees (hard crack stage) and candy is a rich golden color. This entire process should take about 20 minutes.

Pour candy into an 11 x 17-inch non-stick jelly roll pan. Tilt the pan, allowing the candy to spread evenly into all four corners of the pan, then immediately run a knife around the edge of the pan to loosen candy from the sides. The entire surface of the candy should be flat. Cool candy for 3 minutes, then place 1 milk chocolate bar on top. Let candy sit for 5 minutes to allow chocolate to soften and melt, then spread melted chocolate smoothly over surface of the toffee and sprinkle with 1 cup of chopped almonds. Let candy sit for several hours until chocolate is firm.

To spread bottom of candy with chocolate and almonds, first run a knife around the pan to loosen. Place a second 11 x 17-inch jelly roll pan directly on top of original candy pan (rim to rim) then carefully flip the pans, holding them tightly together, so that the candy falls into second pan, chocolate-side-down. Melt second milk chocolate bar in the microwave on defrost for 5 to 7 minutes, then spread on candy and top with remaining 1 cup of chopped almonds. Let candy sit until chocolate becomes firm, then break into chunks.

Some Advice from the Field

*The best way to keep children at home
is to make the home atmosphere pleasant—
and to let the air out of the tires.*

—DOROTHY PARKER

The *Weekly Feeder* system makes dinner a savory, healthy experience for family members—and a pleasant, easy task for the cook. On a personal level, it has influenced our household organization and our family interactions in a very positive way.

But admittedly, I stumbled on the *Weekly Feeder* concept without research or calculated thought. Because of that, I knew other "experts" like me—who earned their organizational/parenting stripes in the busy trenches of today's family life—had similarly discovered some savvy, functional, and just plain fun ideas along the way. Ideas like this deserve to be shared.

No double-blind studies were conducted. No statistics were calculated. Research for the following ideas took place in the home offices, bathrooms, kitchens, nurseries, and family rooms of a wonderful contingent of women who generously contributed the household management and parenting tips *that worked for them.* Their ideas are sprinkled throughout the book, and this chapter includes even more valuable hints. It's impossible to read the following list without picking up some ideas that you will want to incorporate into your daily routine. Be my guest!

Keeping a Home Humming
\<Household Management\>

TELEPHONE TIPS

- Keep a spiral notebook by your main phone/answering machine to record messages you wish to keep. Use the cover and front page to write special telephone numbers that you often re-use. As the book fills, use a highlighter to note telephone numbers or addresses that you might need to refer back to.

- Keep pads of paper and pencils or pens by *every* phone and near where you spend most of your time at home so that you can write down messages, add to your "to do" list, or record quick ideas without having to get up and go searching for a pencil.

- Put a ¾-inch piece of velcro next to a wall phone, on the side of your computer, on the cover of the phone book, or even on the dashboard of your car along with a Post-it pad . . . any place where you want to keep a ballpoint pen handy. This same technique can be used to keep a pair of glasses near your phone or computer.

- Keep extra or recently outdated phone directories for schools, clubs, and the community in your car for those on-the-fly cell calls.

LAUNDRY

- By age 10 or 12, kids can be taught to use the washer and dryer and manage their own laundry. This is a good skill for kids to learn, and a timesaver for Mom.

- If you don't have time to fold clothes as they come out of the dryer, lay them flat on the ironing board with socks and underwear on top. When you're ready to fold, the clothes will have ironed themselves!

- Use only one set of sheets for each bed. Wash them once a week and put them right back on the bed. This saves a lot of space, the sheets are always fresh, and you don't have to fold them.

- If your washer and dryer aren't within earshot, set your kitchen/oven timer to go off when the laundry is done.

STORAGE

- Keep a large plastic storage box with two-piece folding lid in the trunk or back of your car so that your rain gear, extra umbrella, or sporting equipment doesn't tumble around.

- If you have a "mud room" entering the kitchen from the outside, have an open wooden locker built in for each family member to store muddy shoes, backpacks, and coats for easy access. If there's room, add an extra locker for your kids' guests.

- Use large storage boxes decorated for each season to store things like home decorating items, linens, books, music, etc., that you use just one time of year.

PHOTOS

- Stacks—or shoeboxes full—of photos and negatives are depressing! Keep an annual album on your desk so that as photos come in, you can place the best ones in the album right away, then record the subject and date of the negatives, and file them immediately.

- Take lots of pictures and when developing film get triplicates. One copy can go in the family album, one in the appropriate child's album, and the third to grandma, or a college student, or on the refrigerator. Duplicates are very inexpensive compared to reprints.

- Another idea is to have all photos developed in 5 x 7-inch size. The difference in cost is negligible, and you can put the pictures in a frame and change them as often as you want without having to make an extra trip to have a negative enlarged.

MANAGING HOUSEHOLD INFORMATION

- Instead of keeping addresses and telephone numbers in a handwritten book by the telephone, use a spreadsheet program such as Excel to enter alphabetically and numerically sort and update information as needed. Hard copies can then be placed in a binder by the phone.

- Keep a list of all current repair people, electricians, plumbers, etc. Don't forget to leave the list with anyone who may housesit or stay in your house. Let your children know where the list is kept in case there's a household emergency when you're away from home.

- Keep files for your family's personal business close at hand and go through the files weekly. Categories could include: "Correspondence," "To Read," "To Pay," "To Call," "Immediate," "Pending," and "Invitations."

- Here's a comprehensive way to manage all important household information: (1) In an 8 x 10-inch "Week at a Glance" calendar, keep all daily details of your family life—noting birthdays, classes, meetings, events, etc. Tickets to athletic events and plays are clipped to that week, plus any materials or notices pertaining to specific events. Include a list of calls to make and things to do, which are either checked off or re-listed for the following week. Each weekend, review the upcoming week or two and add appropriate items. (2) In a 3 x 5-inch file box keep "monthly" cards and "alphabetical" cards. The monthly cards note the date and cost of household projects as they're completed, suggested upcoming things to do in the yard, when to have windows cleaned, plus Christmas reminders or gift ideas, etc. The alphabetical cards list banking information, credit card numbers, emergency information, social security numbers, etc. (3) In a huge notebook, maintain sections pertaining to homeowners, life, and medical insurance, with the names of your representatives. An emergency section is also helpful in this notebook.

- To keep track of kids' school activities, carpools, after-school classes, lessons or teams, and medical information, keep a 3-ring binder for each child. Use dividers for sections as needed. All the necessary information will be instantly at your fingertips.

- To remember to do those chores done only occasionally, make a chart for the year and assign a room or a special project in each room to a given week. You can do everything from repotting plants to finding the right picture frame, to flipping mattresses or washing throw rugs.

- Keep a "master" grocery list in the kitchen to check off staple items when you run out of them. It helps to do this when you need an item rather than waiting until grocery day to try to remember what you're out of.

- Keep an ongoing blank list in the kitchen/desk area available to the whole family. This list is for anything anyone wants or needs—from personal items to special food items, etc.

- Keep a file just for the house, with ideas for decorating, home improvements, names of recommended workers, etc., easy to find.

- Buy next year's calendar in July or August so you can jot down dates when they are first mentioned.

MAIL

- Sort mail the minute you get it from the mailbox. Stand at the recycle bin and throw the ads, flyers, etc., that you don't want to read right into the waste to save clutter and time.

- Keep a wicker basket near your mail slot. When catalogs arrive that you want to skim, put them into the basket—ready to accompany you to appointments where you may have to wait.

PLANTS

- To keep cut flowers fresh, place a few drops of household bleach (without soap) into the vase before adding cut flowers. The bleach will keep the water clear and will kill any bacteria that may cause flowers to tire or die early.

- To save watering time, only buy plants that are drought resistant, such as ficus, sheflera, grapevine, or other thick, waxy-leafed plants. These plants are flexible in their need for water and can go without watering from one to three weeks without losing their beauty.

- Mix silk flowers and real flowers in large arrangements. It's hard to tell which is which and silk flowers are a great filler.

Making a Plan of Your Own

Home is where one starts from.

—T. S. ELIOT

Making a Plan of Your Own

This meal-planning system has worked well for me for twelve years. During that time I've added some new recipes, deleted a few old ones, and modified many of the rest to reduce the fat content. But I offer the recipes in this book as merely a starting point for the *Weekly Feeder* system, because the important thing is not *what* you prepare when you use it, but the system itself.

Anyone interested enough in cooking to purchase this cookbook undoubtedly has his or her own favorite recipes, some neatly scribed from neighbors, friends, and family, others recorded on scraps of paper or torn from newspapers and magazines. Until I sat down to actually put this idea on paper, my recipe "file" was an old cardboard box stuffed with a disarray of often illegible recipes. It took me longer to *find* and decipher a recipe than to prepare it. But whether you're someone with an organized binder of neatly typed family favorites tucked in alphabetical order between protective plastic sheets . . . or if your recipes are more randomly "sorted" like mine were, those you cook for would miss eating your familiar specialties.

To get the most timesaving benefit from the *Weekly Feeder* system it's best not to do it halfway. While the recipes can be used individually, it's only when you follow the plan as it was designed that you will experience the real timesaving advantages. However, the system is very flexible and can be personalized to suit your family's specific tastes and preferences by creating some WEEKS of your own.

This chapter will help you do just that, with step-by-step instructions to devise up to four personal WEEKS using your own favorite recipes to create balanced menus and customized grocery lists. It can be a fun process, and family input is recommended. Let your kids request their favorite dinners, or ask their advice on side dishes. Once you've created some WEEKS of your own, you can combine them with original *Weekly Feeder* WEEKS that you particularly enjoy. With your computer and a 3-ring binder you can make a personalized cookbook that will add time, ease, and tradition to your busy life.

Creating your own WEEKS is done in three easy steps. You plan your dinner menus using Chart #1; distribute those menus into WEEKS using Chart #2; and prepare customized grocery lists using Chart #3. Just follow these simple instructions.

CHART #1

Plan Your Dinner Menus

- **List dinner entrees from your own repertoire under the appropriate category of poultry, meat, seafood, or vegetarian.**

  Keep in mind that for each WEEK you create, you'll need *a total of* five entrees. These can be any combination, i.e., two vegetarian, two chicken, and one beef, etc. In other words, if you want to create one personalized WEEK, you need to list *a total of* five entrees among the four categories. You'll need a total of ten entrees for two personalized WEEKS, a total of fifteen entrees for three personalized WEEKS, and so on.

- **Complete each dinner menu by listing the side dishes such as salad, potatoes, or whatever you like to serve with that entree.**

  Keep in mind nutritional balance and preparation time. If an entree is time-consuming to prepare, don't choose a salad with a variety of vegetables to chop or a unique dressing to make from scratch. The emphasis should be on simplicity and ease with fresh, healthy ingredients as you complete your personalized menus. Remember that for a nice presentation, fresh is always best.

CHART #2

Create Your Own WEEKS

- **Distribute the completed dinner menus that you have just devised in the four food categories on Chart #1 into the appropriate number of personalized WEEKS on Chart #2, keeping balance and variety in mind.**

Just as you won't want three seafood entrees in one WEEK, don't put two fairly rich, high-calorie entrees together either. The same goes for recipes that take a little longer to prepare. You may also need to adjust the side dishes to insure variety and interest, as you don't want to serve a tossed green salad every night or a favorite rice dish twice in one WEEK.

CHART #3

Prepare Your Customized Grocery Lists

Go to your cookbook shelf and recipe file to gather together all the recipes for each dinner menu you have created. You're now ready to prepare the grocery lists for your new WEEKS.

- For each entree and side dish you've planned for your first WEEK, read the ingredient list for every recipe, and write down the ingredients and the quantity you'll need in the appropriate food category box on Chart #3. If the ingredient is a staple you commonly have on hand, list the ingredient under the "CHECK" designation.

- Complete the process for each of the five menus in your first WEEK; then repeat on a separate Chart #3 for each additional WEEK that you created.

At this point the real work is done. However, it is likely to be in a rough, hand-written form and, if you have access to a computer or word processor, I highly recommend taking the extra time right now to input and save (1) the dinner menu lists for your personal weeks, (2) the grocery lists, and (3) all of the recipes you will be using. Once you've done that, you can print a copy of each and place them together in a handy, organized binder. Extra copies of the grocery lists can be tucked in the binder for your convenience, and you'll avoid the need to search old cookbooks at the most hectic time of day, looking for an elusive recipe. You can also further customize the grocery lists by altering the sequence of ingredients to reflect the layout of your favorite local market.

Having the recipes and grocery lists for your personal system saved on a computer will make it easy for you to continue using the *Weekly Feeder* system in the months and years to come. You can make changes as your family's tastes mature, or as you experiment with new recipes and develop new family favorites.

Now, one more reminder: Don't forget to spend the time you're going to save wisely. Exercise. Take a walk in the rain. Teach your child a card game or invite your neighbors over for dinner. Relax. Enjoy. And keep things simple.

Chart #1   Dinner Menus

Poultry Entrees

Entree: Side Dishes:
Entree: Side Dishes:
Entree: Side Dishes:
Entree: Side Dishes:
Entree: Side Dishes:
Entree: Side Dishes:
Entree: Side Dishes:
Entree: Side Dishes:

Meat Entrees

Entree: Side Dishes:
Entree: Side Dishes:
Entree: Side Dishes:
Entree: Side Dishes:
Entree: Side Dishes:
Entree: Side Dishes:
Entree: Side Dishes:
Entree: Side Dishes:

Chart #1 Dinner Menus

Seafood Entrees

Entree:

Side Dishes:

Entree:

Side Dishes:

Entree:

Side Dishes:

Entree:

Side Dishes:

Entree:

Side Dishes:

Entree:

Side Dishes:

Entree:

Side Dishes:

Entree:

Side Dishes:

Vegetarian Entrees

Entree:

Side Dishes:

Entree:

Side Dishes:

Entree:

Side Dishes:

Entree:

Side Dishes:

Entree:

Side Dishes:

Entree:

Side Dishes:

Entree:

Side Dishes:

Entree:

Side Dishes:

Chart #2 Create Your Own Weeks

Menus for Week 1   Menus for Week 2

Chart #2 Create Your Own Weeks

Menus for Week 3

Menus for Week 4

Chart #3   Groceries for Week 1

Meat/Seafood/Poultry	Staples to Check:
Dairy Products	
Pasta, Tortillas, Rice	
Canned, Frozen	
Vegetables	
Fruits	
Bread	

Chart #3   Groceries for Week 2

Meat/Seafood/Poultry	Staples to Check:
Dairy Products	
Pasta, Tortillas, Rice	
Canned, Frozen	
Vegetables	
Fruits	
Bread	

Chart #3   Groceries for Week 3

Meat/Seafood/Poultry	Staples to Check:
Dairy Products	
Pasta, Tortillas, Rice	
Canned, Frozen	
Vegetables	
Fruits	
Bread	

Chart #3   Groceries for Week 4

Meat/Seafood/Poultry	Staples to Check:
Dairy Products	
Pasta, Tortillas, Rice	
Canned, Frozen	
Vegetables	
Fruits	
Bread	

Grocery Lists

Life is too short to stuff a mushroom.

—SHIRLEY CONRAN

Week 1 Groceries

- [ ] 1½   pound flank steak
- [ ] ½   pound lean bacon
- [ ] 16   boneless, skinned chicken breasts
- [ ] 1   pound cooked baby shrimp

- [ ] 5   ounces grated Parmesan cheese
- [ ] 2   9-ounce packages fresh spaghetti
- [ ] 2   9-ounce packages fresh linguini
- [ ] 2   9-ounce packages fresh angel hair pasta

- [ ] 1   bottle Caesar salad dressing
- [ ] 1   8-ounce can tomato sauce

- [ ] 1   16-ounce can corn
- [ ] 1   14½-ounce can tomato pieces
- [ ] 2   14½-ounce cans chicken broth
- [ ] ½   pint light sour cream

- [ ] 2   heads garlic
- [ ] 1   large onion
- [ ] 2   heads lettuce or romaine
- [ ] 4   large tomatoes
- [ ] 1   bunch green onions
- [ ] 1   large bunch broccoli
- [ ] 1   green pepper
- [ ] 8–10   mushrooms
- [ ] 4   zucchini
- [ ] ½   pound snow peas
- [ ] 1   large bunch grapes
- [ ] 3   oranges
- [ ] 1   small bunch bananas
- [ ] 1   apple

- [ ] 1   package bread sticks
- [ ] 1   loaf French bread

Check:

- [ ] basil
- [ ] butter/margarine
- [ ] chicken bouillon
- [ ] crushed red pepper
- [ ] garlic powder
- [ ] ground ginger
- [ ] honey
- [ ] marjoram
- [ ] olive oil
- [ ] oregano
- [ ] raw rice
- [ ] salad dressing
- [ ] salt and fresh ground black pepper
- [ ] sherry
- [ ] soy sauce
- [ ] thyme
- [ ] vegetable oil
- [ ] vinegar

Week 2 Groceries

❑	1	pound leanest ground beef
❑	1	pound sirloin steak
❑	½	pound ham, cooked turkey, or turkey ham
❑	4	boneless, skinned chicken breasts
❑	⅔–¾	pound halibut or cod fillets
❑	2	9-ounce packages fresh fettuccine
❑	2	9-ounce packages angel hair pasta
❑	1	28-ounce can Italian-style tomatoes
❑	1	14½-ounce can tomato pieces
❑	1	10¾-ounce can tomato puree
❑	1	15½-ounce can corn
❑	1	6-ounce jar marinated artichoke hearts
❑	1	15½-ounce can dark red kidney beans
❑	2	14½-ounce cans beef broth
❑	4	ounces Cheddar cheese
❑	½	pint light sour cream
❑	1	head garlic
❑	4	large sweet onions
❑	1	head lettuce or romaine
❑	1	large bunch green onions
❑	1	bunch parsley
❑	8	mushrooms
❑	1	small red bell pepper
❑	3–4	medium zucchini
❑	1	bunch broccoli
❑	2	carrots
❑	1	honeydew melon
❑	6	oranges
❑	1	small bunch grapes
❑	1	small bunch bananas
❑	1	green apple
❑	1	loaf French bread

Check:

- [ ] basil
- [ ] butter/margarine
- [ ] cornstarch
- [ ] cumin
- [ ] Dijon mustard
- [ ] eggs
- [ ] ketchup
- [ ] light soy sauce
- [ ] olive oil
- [ ] oregano
- [ ] raw rice
- [ ] salad dressing
- [ ] salt and fresh ground black pepper
- [ ] sesame oil
- [ ] sherry
- [ ] soy sauce
- [ ] vegetable oil
- [ ] white wine

Week 3 Groceries

- [ ] 1 pound lean ground beef
- [ ] 1¼ pound sirloin steak
- [ ] 10–12 boneless, skinned chicken thighs
- [ ] 2 pounds sole fillets
- [ ] 8 boneless, skinned chicken breasts

- [ ] 10 8-inch flour tortillas
- [ ] 2 9-ounce packages fresh spaghetti

- [ ] 5 ounces grated Parmesan cheese
- [ ] 1 26-ounce jar spaghetti sauce
- [ ] 1 small can green chiles
- [ ] ½ pint light sour cream
- [ ] ½ pint heavy cream
- [ ] 3 14½-ounce cans chicken broth
- [ ] 1 3-ounce package slivered almonds

- [ ] 1 head garlic
- [ ] 2 large onions
- [ ] 1 large bunch green onions
- [ ] 1 head lettuce or romaine
- [ ] 3 medium Roma tomatoes
- [ ] 1 large avocado
- [ ] 1 bunch parsley
- [ ] 1 bunch cilantro
- [ ] 12 mushrooms
- [ ] 10 cherry tomatoes
- [ ] 4 baking potatoes
- [ ] 1 cup bean sprouts
- [ ] 1 pound snow peas
- [ ] 1 red bell pepper
- [ ] 6 medium carrots
- [ ] 1 small bunch celery
- [ ] 1 large bunch broccoli
- [ ] 1 zucchini
- [ ] 1 large lime

Week 3 Groceries *(continued)*

- [ ] 1   honeydew melon
- [ ] 1   lemon

- [ ] 1   loaf French bread
- [ ] 1   loaf focaccia bread

Check:

- [ ] brown sugar
- [ ] butter/margarine
- [ ] cornstarch
- [ ] cumin
- [ ] dry bread crumbs
- [ ] flour
- [ ] olive oil
- [ ] raw rice
- [ ] salad dressing
- [ ] salt and fresh ground black pepper
- [ ] sesame oil
- [ ] sherry
- [ ] soy sauce
- [ ] toasted sesame seeds
- [ ] vegetable oil

Week 4 Groceries

- [ ] ½ pound lean bacon
- [ ] 1 large fresh turkey breast (approximately 1 pound)
- [ ] 1½ pound flank steak
- [ ] 4 boneless, skinned chicken breasts

- [ ] 1 16-ounce package Marco Polo Chinese noodles
- [ ] 1 16-ounce package Chinese egg noodles
- [ ] 2 9-ounce packages fresh linguini
- [ ] 2 9-ounce packages angel hair pasta

- [ ] 5 ounces grated Parmesan cheese
- [ ] 2 6-ounce cans lump crab meat (no leg meat)
- [ ] 1 3-ounce package sliced almonds
- [ ] 1 package bulgar wheat
- [ ] 3 14½-ounce cans chicken broth

- [ ] 1 head garlic
- [ ] 3 heads lettuce or romaine
- [ ] 3 bunches green onions
- [ ] 3 medium ripe tomatoes
- [ ] 2 onions
- [ ] 1 bunch parsley
- [ ] 1 small bunch celery
- [ ] 1 green pepper
- [ ] 10 mushrooms
- [ ] 1 large bunch broccoli
- [ ] 8 large carrots
- [ ] 3 large oranges
- [ ] 1 lemon
- [ ] 1 pineapple
- [ ] 3 green apples

- [ ] 1 loaf French bread

Check:

- [ ] brown sugar
- [ ] butter/margarine
- [ ] chicken bouillon
- [ ] cornstarch
- [ ] eggs
- [ ] garlic salt
- [ ] light soy sauce
- [ ] oyster sauce
- [ ] salad dressing
- [ ] salt and fresh ground black pepper
- [ ] sesame oil
- [ ] sherry
- [ ] soy sauce
- [ ] teriyaki sauce
- [ ] toasted sesame seeds
- [ ] vegetable oil

Week 5 Groceries

- ☐ ¾   pound baby shrimp
- ☐ 1¼   pound flank steak
- ☐ 1   pound fresh ground turkey
- ☐ 12   boneless, skinned chicken breasts

- ☐ 2   9-ounce packages fresh linguini
- ☐ 2   9-ounce packages fresh spaghetti
- ☐ 1   16-ounce package Marco Polo Chinese noodles

- ☐ 5   ounces grated Parmesan cheese
- ☐ 1   small container prepared pesto sauce
- ☐ 1   28-ounce can Italian-style tomatoes
- ☐ 1   6-ounce can tomato paste

- ☐ ½   pint light sour cream
- ☐ 1   10-ounce package frozen spinach

- ☐ 1   head garlic
- ☐ 2   heads lettuce or romaine
- ☐ 2   bunches green onions
- ☐ 2   onions
- ☐ 10   cherry tomatoes
- ☐ 1   bunch parsley
- ☐ 1   red bell pepper
- ☐ 1   small zucchini
- ☐ 4   baking potatoes
- ☐ 2   carrots
- ☐ 2   dozen mushrooms
- ☐ 1   large head bok choy
- ☐ 1   orange
- ☐ 1   pineapple
- ☐ ¼   watermelon

- ☐ 1   package bread sticks

Check:

- [ ] basil
- [ ] bay leaf
- [ ] butter/margarine
- [ ] cornstarch
- [ ] curry powder
- [ ] honey
- [ ] milk
- [ ] olive oil
- [ ] oregano
- [ ] prepared mustard
- [ ] raw rice
- [ ] rosemary
- [ ] salad dressing
- [ ] salt and fresh ground black pepper
- [ ] sherry
- [ ] soy sauce
- [ ] sugar
- [ ] vegetable oil
- [ ] white wine

Week 6 Groceries

- ❑ 12   boneless, skinned chicken breasts
- ❑ 1   pound flank steak
- ❑ 1   pound leanest ground beef
- ❑ ¼   pound fresh baby shrimp

- ❑ 2   9-ounce packages fresh angel hair pasta
- ❑ 12   ounces dry spaghetti

- ❑ 5   ounces grated Parmesan cheese
- ❑ 2   6-ounce cans lump crab meat (no leg meat)
- ❑ 10–12   taco shells
- ❑ 1   package taco sauce mix
- ❑ 3–4   ounces Cheddar cheese
- ❑ ½   cup dry-roasted cashews
- ❑ ½   pint light sour cream
- ❑ ½   pint half 'n' half
- ❑ 1   10-ounce package frozen peas

- ❑ 1   head garlic
- ❑ 3   heads lettuce or romaine
- ❑ 2   bunches green onions
- ❑ 1   tomato
- ❑ 3   Roma tomatoes
- ❑ 2   onions
- ❑ 1   red pepper
- ❑ 6–8   red-skinned potatoes
- ❑ 8   mushrooms
- ❑ 1   large bunch broccoli
- ❑ 1   large leek
- ❑ ½   head cabbage
- ❑ 1   bunch celery
- ❑ 1   avocado
- ❑ 1   lemon
- ❑ 5   large oranges
- ❑ 1   bunch grapes
- ❑ 1   cantaloupe, casaba, or honeydew melon
- ❑ 1   bunch bananas

- ❑ 1   loaf French bread

Check:

- [ ] butter/margarine
- [ ] chicken bouillon
- [ ] cornstarch
- [ ] crushed red pepper
- [ ] dry bread crumbs
- [ ] eggs
- [ ] garlic powder
- [ ] light soy sauce
- [ ] Madeira
- [ ] oregano
- [ ] raw rice
- [ ] salad dressing
- [ ] salt and fresh ground black pepper
- [ ] sherry
- [ ] soy sauce
- [ ] sugar
- [ ] vegetable oil
- [ ] white wine
- [ ] whole black peppercorns

Week 7 Groceries

- [ ] 3½–5 pound whole fryer roaster chicken
- [ ] 6 large country-style pork spareribs
- [ ] 4 boneless, skinned chicken breasts
- [ ] 8 ounces smoked turkey sausage
- [ ] 1¼ pounds large shrimp

- [ ] 1 16-ounce package dry orzo pasta
- [ ] 6 ounces dry capellini
- [ ] 1 16-ounce package Arborio rice
- [ ] 1 16-ounce package couscous
- [ ] 1 package cornbread mix

- [ ] 5 ounces grated Parmesan cheese
- [ ] 4 ounces feta cheese
- [ ] ½ pint heavy cream

- [ ] 1 49½-ounce can chicken broth
- [ ] 2 28-ounce cans whole tomatoes
- [ ] 1 10-ounce package frozen peas
- [ ] 1 10-ounce package frozen spinach
- [ ] 1 8.5-ounce jar sun-dried tomatoes, packed in oil

- [ ] 2 large onions
- [ ] 1 small shallot
- [ ] 2 heads garlic
- [ ] ¼ cup fresh basil
- [ ] 4 tomatoes
- [ ] 1 head Swiss chard
- [ ] 1 carrot
- [ ] 1 bunch parsley
- [ ] 2 heads lettuce or romaine
- [ ] 1 large bunch green onions
- [ ] 1 small bunch grapes
- [ ] 1 banana
- [ ] 1 apple
- [ ] 2 oranges
- [ ] ½ cantaloupe
- [ ] 2 lemons

- ☐ 1 package pita bread
- ☐ 1 loaf French bread

Check:

- ☐ brown sugar
- ☐ butter/margarine
- ☐ celery seed
- ☐ chili powder
- ☐ honey
- ☐ ketchup
- ☐ olive oil
- ☐ salad dressing
- ☐ salt and fresh ground black pepper
- ☐ sherry
- ☐ thyme
- ☐ white wine
- ☐ Worcestershire sauce

Week 8 Groceries

- [ ] 1½   pound flank steak
- [ ] 1   pound large shrimp
- [ ] 4   boneless, skinned chicken breasts
- [ ] 4   inch-thick halibut steaks
- [ ] 2   large pork tenderloins

- [ ] 1   16-ounce package Marco Polo Chinese noodles
- [ ] 1   8-ounce package wild rice
- [ ] 1   16-ounce package brown rice
- [ ] 2   9-ounce packages fresh linguini
- [ ] 2   9-ounce packages fresh angel hair pasta

- [ ] 5   ounces grated Parmesan cheese
- [ ] 4   ounces feta cheese
- [ ] ½   pint heavy cream

- [ ] 1   6-ounce can tomato paste
- [ ] 3   14½-ounce cans chicken broth
- [ ] 1   15½-ounce can black beans
- [ ] 1   17-ounce can pineapple tidbits
- [ ] 1   10-ounce package currants
- [ ] 1   3-ounce package chopped walnuts
- [ ] 1   8.5-ounce jar sun-dried tomatoes, packed in oil
- [ ] 1   small bag sun-dried tomatoes (dry, in bag)

- [ ] 1   pound fresh green beans
- [ ] 2   large, sweet onions
- [ ] 14   Roma tomatoes
- [ ] 3   red bell peppers
- [ ] 1   yellow pepper
- [ ] 4   bunches green onions
- [ ] 3–4   shiitake mushrooms
- [ ] 1   small chunk fresh ginger
- [ ] 3   heads garlic
- [ ] 6   mushrooms
- [ ] 1   bunch parsley
- [ ] 2   heads lettuce or romaine
- [ ] ¼   cup fresh basil

Index

Other Books by Starburst Publishers

The Weekly Feeder—*Cori Kirkpatrick*

Subtitled: *A Revolutionary Shopping, Cooking, and Meal-Planning System*

The Weekly Feeder is a revolutionary meal-planning system that will make preparing home-cooked dinners more convenient than ever. At the beginning of each week, simply choose one of the eight preplanned weekly menus, tear out the corresponding grocery list, do your shopping, and whip up a great meal in less than 45 minutes! The author's household management tips, equipment checklists, and nutrition information make this system a must for any busy family. Included with every recipe is a personal anecdote from the author emphasizing the importance of good food, a healthy family, and a well-balanced life.

(trade paper) ISBN 1892016095   **$16.95**

The World's Oldest Health Plan—*Kathleen O'Bannon Baldinger*

Subtitled: *Health, Nutrition and Healing from the Bible.* Offers a complete health plan for body, mind and spirit, just as Jesus did. It includes programs for diet, exercise and mental health. Contains foods and recipes to lower cholesterol and blood pressure, improve the immune system and other bodily functions, reduce stress, reduce or cure constipation, eliminate insomnia, reduce forgetfulness, confusion and anger, increase circulation and thinking ability, eliminate "yeast" problems, improve digestion, and much more.

(trade paper) ISBN 0914984578   **$14.95**

More of Him, Less of Me—*Jan Christensen*

Subtitled: *A Daybook of My Personal Insights, Inspirations & Meditations on the Weigh Down™ Diet.* The insight shared in this year-long daybook of inspiration will encourage you on your weight-loss journey, bring you to a deeper relationship with God, and help you improve any facet of your life. Each page includes an essay, scripture, and a tip-of-the-day that will encourage and uplift you as you trust God to help you achieve your proper weight. Perfect companion guide for anyone on the Weigh Down™ diet!

(cloth) ISBN 1892016001   **$17.95**

Desert Morsels—*Jan Christiansen*

Subtitled: *A Journal with Encouraging Tidbits from My Journey on the Weigh Down™ Diet.* When Jan Christiansen set out to lose weight on the Weigh Down™ Diet she got more than she bargained for! In addition to losing over 35 pounds and gaining a closer relationship with God, Jan discovered a gift—her ability to entertain and comfort fellow dieters! Jan's inspiring website led to the release of her best-selling first book, *More of Him, Less of Me.* Now, Jan serves another helping of her wit and *His* wisdom in this lovely companion journal. Includes inspiring scripture, insightful comments, stories from readers, room for the reader's personal reflection and *Plenty of **Attitude** (p-attitude).*

(cloth) ISBN 1892016214   **$17.95**

The Bible—God's Word for the Biblically-Inept™—*Larry Richards*

An excellent book to start learning the entire Bible. Get the basics or the in-depth information you are seeking with this user-friendly overview. From Creation to Christ to the Millennium, learning the Bible has never been easier.

(trade paper) ISBN 0914984551 **$16.95**

Health & Nutrition—God's Word for the Biblically-Inept™
—*Kathleen O'Bannon Baldinger*

The Bible is full of God's rules for good health! Baldinger reveals scientific evidence that proves the diet and health principles outlined in the Bible are the best for total health. Learn about the Bible Diet, the food pyramid, and fruits and vegetables from the Bible! Experts include: Pamela Smith, Julian Whitaker, Kenneth Cooper, and T. D. Jakes.

(trade paper) ISBN 0914984055 **$16.95**

God Stories—*Donna I. Douglas*

Subtitled: *They're So Amazing, Only God Could Make Them Happen*

Famous individuals share their personal, true-life experiences with God in this beautiful new book! Find out how God has touched the lives of top recording artists, professional athletes, and other newsmakers like Jessi Colter, Deana Carter, Ben Vereen, Stephanie Zimbalist, Cindy Morgan, Sheila E., Joe Jacoby, Cheryl Landon, Brett Butler, Clifton Taulbert, Babbie Mason, Michael Medved, Sandi Patty, Charlie Daniels, and more! Their stories are intimate, poignant, and sure to inspire and motivate you as you listen for God's message in your own life!

(cloth) ISBN 1892016117 **$18.95**

Allergy Cooking With Ease—*Nicolette M. Dumke*

Subtitled: *The No Wheat, Milk, Eggs, Corn, Soy, Yeast, Sugar, Grain, and Gluten Cookbook.*

A book designed to provide a wide variety of recipes to meet many different dietary and social needs, and whenever possible, save you time in food preparation. Includes recipes for foods that food allergy patients think they will never eat again, as well as time saving tricks and an Allergen Avoidance index.

(trade paper) ISBN 091498442X **$14.95**

Purchasing Information:
www.starburstpublishers.com

Books are available from your favorite bookstore, either from current stock or special order. To assist bookstore in locating your selection be sure to give title, author, and ISBN #. If unable to purchase from the bookstore you may order direct from STARBURST PUBLISHERS. When ordering enclose full payment plus shipping and handling as follows: Post Office (4th Class)—$3.00 (Up to $20.00), $4.00 ($20.01–$50.00), 8% ($50.01 and Up); UPS—$4.50 (Up to $20.00), $6.00 ($20.01–$50.00), 12% ($50.01 and Up); Canada—$5.00 (Up to $35.00), 15% ($35.01 and Up); Overseas (Surface)—$5.00 (Up to $25.00), 20% ($25.01 and Up). Payment in U.S. Funds only. Please allow two to three weeks minimum (longer overseas) for delivery. Make checks payable to and mail to: STARBURST PUBLISHERS, P.O. BOX 4123, LANCASTER, PA 17604. Credit card orders may also be placed by calling 1-800-441-1456 (credit card orders only), Mon–Fri, 8:30 A.M. to 5:30 P.M. Eastern Standard Time. Prices subject to change without notice. Catalog available for a 9 x 12 self-addressed envelope with 4 first-class stamps.

Your Personal Cooking Journal

Your Personal Cooking Journal

_____

_____

_____

_____

_____

_____

_____

_____

_____

_____

_____

_____

_____

_____

_____

_____

_____

_____

Your Personal Cooking Journal

Your Personal Cooking Journal

Your Personal Cooking Journal

Your Personal Cooking Journal

Your Personal Cooking Journal

_____
_____
_____
_____
_____
_____
_____
_____
_____
_____
_____
_____
_____
_____
_____
_____
_____
_____
_____
_____

Your Personal Cooking Journal